Writing Nowhere

A Beginner's Guide to Utopia

Rowan B. Fortune

GW00371219

DOWN DEEP BOOKS

Published by Down Deep Books
an imprint of Cinnamon Press

Based in Scrignac, France, and Warwickshire, England.
Administrative office: Office 49019, PO Box 15113 , Birmingham, B2
2NJ
www.cinnamonpress.com

ISBN: 978-1-78864-803-5

British Library Cataloguing in Publication Data. A CIP record for
this book can be obtained from the British Library.

Designed and typeset by Cinnamon Press.

Cinnamon Press is represented in the UK by Inpress Ltd.

Acknowledgements

I would like to thank Professor Ian Gregson, Professor Helen Wilcox,
Dr Kachi Ozumba, Dr Zoë Skoulding, my wife, Nina Anana, Dr.
Angela Cotter, my mother, Dr Jan Fortune, and friend, Ann Drysdale,
for their contributions and assistance to the portion of the text
extracted from my PhD. For their contributions to my utopian
timeline, I thank David Pavett and Liza Daly. I would like to thank
Adam Craig and Dr Jan Fortune for eding and formatting this book
and its ebook edition and Adam for the wonderful cover. All errors
contained within the text are entirely mine.

CONTENTS

Writing Nowhere

Foreword

Utopia is a double entendre: the Greek etymology (no place) and the homophone eu-topia (good place) play into its contested quality as a floating signifier.[1] Utopia can suggest certain movements and fictions as well as anti-utopian rhetoric, such as in Marx's comment that 'Communism is for us not a *state of affairs* which is to be established, an *ideal* to which reality [will] have to adjust[…]'.[2] The dialectical antonym of utopia, dystopia, is even more indefinite: a place, a bad place? Both utopia and dystopia open psychogeographical counterfactuals, alternative worlds—providing commentaries and experimental spaces for their readers. Both blur into one another; for instance, is Thomas More's *Utopia*[3] (1516) satirical, an anti-utopia prefiguring dystopia, or a blueprint? Is dystopia analogous to tragedy and utopia to comedy, or does this separation fail to recognise a more indistinct boundary—a Heraclitean unity of opposites? This ambiguity reaches through the practice of utopic and dystopic fictions.

The opacity of genres such as utopia and dystopia goes further. Fátima Vieira notes that utopia has spawned 'words such as eutopia, dystopia, anti-utopia, alotopia, euchronia, heterotopia, ecotopia and hyperutopia'.[4] There is a need, for the purpose of study, to give specificity to the concept by providing tighter definitions. However, before such a definition can be advanced, it is necessary to outline some of the limits and challenges presented by defining a literary genre.

Anis S. Bawarshi and Mary Jo Reiff define 'genre',

including within the context of a literary tradition, as 'a typified way of recognising, responding to, acting meaningfully and consequentially within, and thus participating in the reproduction of, recurring situations'. While it is not within my scope to give an analysis of genre, it will become evident that my approach assumes a non-traditional perspective, understanding, with Reiff and Bawarshi, that genre encompasses

> knowledge of what and whose purposes genres serve; how to negotiate one's intentions in relation to genres' social expectations and motives; when and why and where to use genres; what reader/writer relationships genre maintain; and how genres relate to other genres in the coordination of social life.[5]

Using examples from cross-genres, Margaret Atwood argues that 'when it comes to genres, the borders are increasingly undefended, and things slip back and forth across them with insouciance.'[6] I am unsure whether or not this is true, and if it is true, whether it is newly so. Irrespective, for the purposes of this analysis it is useful to be more methodologically precise with a definition that limits the scope of what can be called a utopia.

Similarly, while intertextuality (a concept that informs looser conceptions of genre) is acknowledged in the background of any critical reading of the utopian tradition, it is not applicable to advancing a more precise study. Roland Barthes defines intertextuality not as an attempt 'to find the "sources", [and] the "influences" of a work', but as the 'anonymous, untraceable, and yet *already read*'[7] network that encompasses all text. For Barthes intertextuality is the fact of every text existing in a continuum of texts, a totality that cannot be demarcated or fully mapped.

It is vital to have a working idea of what constitutes a utopia to meaningfully explore its history. Making allowances for Michel Foucault's *episteme*, 'the totality of relations that can be discovered'[8], relevant, intertextual material is inexhaustible for this (or any) genre. As Nicole Pohl describes utopia, it is 'indebted to classical utopianism, early-modern travel writing, the pastoral/Arcadian tradition and finally Christian Chiliasm.'[9] Beginning with More's *Utopia* allows us to narrow our survey to something more manageable, but when it comes to providing a brief chronology of utopia I will also show that my choice of texts is not arbitrary. Before such a chronology, it will nonetheless be worth outlining some notable novels on the boundaries too—thereby sketching some ambiguous and adjacent genres, and suggesting that a genre, in the sense I am using it, is a helpful tool for guiding investigation and perhaps nothing more.

According to J. C. Davis, as summarised by Susan Bruce, a useful typology of five ideal-world genres can help us to identify the key features of the utopia. The main distinction is about how the author of a given story decides to negotiate the

> gap between supply and demand. *The Land of Cockaygne*, he argues, assumes unlimited abundance in order to fulfil unlimited desire. The Arcadia fuses a less excessive natural abundance with a representation of a humanity less acquisitive and more easily satisfied than 'real' human beings would be. The Perfect Moral Commonwealth realizes its ideal through an idealization of the nature of humanity. In Millennial literature parity between desire and available material wealth is effected by a *deus ex machina*, whose intervention transforms both man and nature.[10]

Bruce summarises Davis's fifth type as utopianism, in which organisation is privileged:

> the utopianist devises bureaucratic and institutional systems in order to contain desire and transgression, and thus to apportion a limited supply of material satisfactions. (xiii)

One benefit of Davis's approach to the genre, and to pursuing his fifth type of what I will coin 'institutional utopia', is to correct what Vieira identifies as a misconception, that utopia be equated with perfection.[11] This is not without contention. Krishan Kumar, for example, argues that perfectibility is central to utopia, although he softens that view with a caveat on human nature; the type of perfection must be 'qualified—but not too much—by something like the belief in original sin.'[12] Whether 'sin' is conceived as the total depravity of Augustinian Protestantism or moderated by freewill in Catholic theology, it remains a substantial stipulation. Here again, institutional checks to human evil are considered paramount. Karl Mannheim thus offers an alternative to perfection and provides a more adaptable definition in which utopia merely eliminates 'the order of things prevailing at the time.'[13] Nonetheless, what Kumar's thesis does usefully show is how ideal societies overlap:

> Paradise is fused with the Golden Age; Cockaygne is a reproach to Arcadia while it borrows heavily from the Golden Age and Paradise; the Millennium is paradise restored; the ideal city draws upon the myths of ancient Golden Age civilizations.

All of these types have political dimensions, yet as Kumar's thinking indicates, only the fifth category of utopia (institutional utopia) definitively addresses its audience through narrative: 'Fictive elements no doubt have a role to play in these modes but in none of them is narrative fiction, as in the utopia, the defining form.'[14] Atwood agrees with the importance of fiction for the utopia when she distinguishes between the genre proper and later novels that merely entertain utopian thought: 'Ideas about—for instance—untried forms of social organization are introduced, if at all, through conversations among characters or in the form of diary or reverie, rather than being dramatized, as they are in the utopia and the dystopia.'[15]

Both Kumar and I locate the beginning of the genre as a meaningful tradition with More, but Kumar goes further. He denies any prior examples to More and adds the claim that the form is uniquely Western: 'Utopia is a secular variety of social thought. It is a creation of Renaissance humanism.'[16] Nonetheless, earlier non-European works, for instance Tao Yuanming's poem 'Peach Blossom Springs', written between the third and forth centuries EC, complicate the Eurocentric picture. Yuanming's ideal society has narrative, which means it meets Kumar's criteria for belonging to utopia:

> And the path they trod was covered with grass
> and deserted.
> And the living they gain is by tilling the soil
> and reaping;
> When the sun goes down they go to rest
> together.
> Bamboo and mulberry blend to give them
> shade,
> Beans and rice follow at seasons due.
> From the spring silkworm they gather long
> thread,
> At the autumn harvest there is no imperial
> tax.[17]

Although 'Peach Blossom Springs' is a fiction about a perfect society, its narrative is sketchy and it arguably fails to meet Davis's criteria as it includes elements of Cockaygne, such as the eternally good harvests and convenient foliage. Moreover, since this essay begins with More, the predominant focus will be Western.

The working definition of utopia for the purposes of our critical discussion, then, is a fictional account of a society with limited resources that strives towards a social ideal. Without these stipulations many arguments could be made for including earlier texts: Plato's *Republic* (c. BCE 380)[18], Tacitus *Germanica* (c. 98)[19] and Plutarch's *Life of Lycurgus* (c. 100)[20]. St. Augustine's *City of God* (c. 400)[21] and Aquinas's commentaries on Aristotle (1272)[22] could be added, with Lyman Tower Sargent arguing that 'Christianity was the fount of Western utopianism'.[23] Quentin Skinner contends that More merely contributed to, rather than initiated, the broad Renaissance debate over the best possible commonwealth.[24] In his biography of More, Peter Berglar looks at the writer's formation and thereby lends credence to Skinner's conjecture: 'While still a student [...More] lectured on St. Augustine's *City of God* at St. Lawrence's'.[25]

Introducing a caveat that would still include a range of utopias within the working definition, without making 'utopia' a ubiquitous and unwieldy category, Kumar similarly narrows the focus of utopian studies by beginning with More. Earlier texts constitute, in his view, 'at most a portrayal of the principles of the ideal state, not an exemplification of those principles in action, in concrete institutions and ways of life.'[26] Kumar demonstrates that the earlier texts foreshadow, but do not fully exemplify, the genre.

In continuing to delimit utopia for the purposes of my essay, Davis's contribution is particularly pertinent to later science fiction. For example, the society of Iain M.

Banks's Culture series is not utopian in this sense as 'the capacity for means of production [...] exceeded every [...] demand its not unimaginative citizens could make.'[27] Post-scarcity novels, which picture societies removed from material constraints by magic or technology, could be said to comprise a genre with roots in Cockaygne myths and folk songs, for example 'The Big Rock Candy Mountain': 'Where the handouts grow on bushes, / And you sleep out every night.'[28] Utopia could be said to be a sub-genre of post-scarcity myths, because it depicts ideal societies but with great limitations on the content of that depiction. Going further, the Cockaygne stories could be described as a more universal, basic idea about a land of plenty from which later, more specific utopia derives. Moreover, the post-scarcity genre can be used to explore interesting ideas in contemporary literature, such as the pitfalls of overabundance. In Samuel R. Delany's Foucaultian *Trouble on Triton: An Ambiguous Heterotopia* (1976) 'they made it so easy for you—all you have to know is what you want'.[29] Nonetheless, difficulties arise precisely from the easiness such abundance affords. Still, as in the following dialogue from *Star Trek*, we see the Cockaygne genre of abundance circumnavigating problems that utopia constitutively confronts:

> Keeve: We live in different universes, you and I. Yours is about diplomacy, politics, strategy. Mine is about blankets! If we were to exchange places for one night, you might better understand.
>
> Picard: Mr. Data, see that the replicators provide a blanket for every man, woman, and child before nightfall.[30]

The character Keeve creates a distinction between the concerns of institutional organisation, relevant to utopias, and the limitless technological possibilities afforded to

Picard by technology. The response given by Picard exemplifies that particular distinction between utopias and this other genre. That is, that the post-scarcity society can ignore social problems that utopias attempt to solve.

We frequently find that the creatures of science fiction have more to do with what could be called archetypes than with science. The archetype of the Golem becomes Mary Shelley's Frankenstein; something like the dynamics of werewolves is replicated (if not also surpassed) by Robert Louis Stevenson's *Strange Case of Dr. Jekyll and Mr. Hyde* (1886); ghosts become people's digitally uploaded consciousness; monsters that filled medieval bestiaries[31] become Kaijū; Blemmyes and Monopods become humanoid mutants, while demons are rendered malevolent AIs as in William Gibson's dystopian *Neuromancer* (1984): 'For thousands of years men have dreamed of pacts with demons. Only now are such things possible.'[32] While the Renaissance utopian genre arguably dwindles, the older Cockaygne narratives flourish under a new guise. This suggests that utopia is a bounded historical (and therefore contingent) phenomenon within the scope of a more universal form of human imagining. There will always be imagined worlds without scarcity (at least, if we don't create such a world), but utopias are given no guarantee of existing.

Despite generally not being considered utopia, science fiction overlaps stylistically with utopia in ways that are important to, and inform, my study here. The theorist of science fiction, Darko Suvin, identifies significant common ground between science fiction and a range of other genres in their reliance on cognitive estrangement. This is true of

> '[...] the classical and medieval "fortunate island" story, the "fabulous voyage" story from antiquity on, the Renaissance and Baroque

"Utopia" and "planetary novel", the Enlightenment "state [political] novel", the modern "anticipation" and "anti-utopia."'[33]

Suvin derives the idea of cognitive estrangement from Bertolt Brecht's verfremdungseffekt and the Russian Formalist Viktor Shklovsky's idea of priem otstranenie. This technique 'consists in turning the object of which one is to be made aware, to which one's attention is to be drawn, from something ordinary, familiar, immediately accessible, into something peculiar, sticking and unexpected'.[34] This makes the reader critically re-evaluate the narrative's content, which is necessary in novels of ideas, especially utopias.

Techniques such as defamiliarisation allow broader utopian themes to be addressed in speculative literature, themes that break the mould by using the fantastical or situating new societies in different times or distant places. Slavoj Žižek singles out Theodore Sturgeon's *More Than Human* (1953),[35] a story about misfits with superpowers forming a gestalt entity, as an example of an allegorical and utopic 'community of freaks'.[36] This arguably falls outside Davis's criteria for 'utopian' writing as members of the parabolic community are inhuman in ways that liberate them from human social needs, but still does so in ways that explore the nature of what it means to be human.

Science fiction 'utopias' are therefore of limited reference as, similarly, are non-western currents in utopian fiction. Whilst Jacqueline Dutton's overview includes: 'the spirit of utopia (Ernest Bloch), the desire for utopia (Ruth Levitas), critical utopias and critical dystopias (Tom Moylan) and utopianism (Krishan Kumar).'[37] These approaches lose the discriminatory advantages of the tighter definition I am outlining. This definition does not reflect any criticism of excluded works of literature, but merely focusses the essay to cover a more manageable field of texts.

The idea of the utopia as a post-apocalyptic genre furnishes other borderline cases: E. M. Forster's *The Machine Stops* (1909)[38] is a prescient look at environmental catastrophe and technological enslavement; John Wyndham's *The Chrysalids* (1955)[39] combines utopian and dystopian motifs; both Walter M. Miller, Jr.'s *A Canticle for Leibowitz* (1960)[40] and Russell Hoban's *Riddley Walker* (1980)[41] look at how societies reconstitute histories after nuclear devastation, while Atwood's three twenty-first century novels *Oryx and Crake* (2003), *The Year of the Flood* (2009) and *MaddAddam* (2013)[42] explore similar arenas. Dmitry Glukhovsky's *Metro 2033* (2005),[43] Sheri S. Tepper's *The Gate to Women's Country* (1988)[44] and Mary Shelley's *The Last Man* (1826)[45] are radically varied liminal examples of post-apocalypse fiction, but all are concerned with disaster and, pertinently, the inadequacies and dangers of ideal world projects.

There is not enough space, either, to reflect in depth on utopian movements or theories, both in terms of their texts and as a form of political practice, which constitute various related genres conveyed in different forms for conflicting ideologies: be that Republican, early Liberalism, Anarchism or those Engels dubbed utopian socialism.[46] Thomas Hobbes's *Leviathan* (1651),[47] Gerrard Winstanley's *The Law of Freedom in a Platform Or True Magistracie Restored* (1652)[48] and John Locke's *A Letter Concerning Toleration* (1689)[49] are political documents written in the aftermath of the English Civil War, which also produced literary utopias engaging in the same debates about legitimate governance, such as James Harrington's *The Commonwealth of Oceana (*1656).[50]

Edmund Burke's *Reflections on the Revolution in France* (1790)[51] espouses anti-utopian ideas against the change wrought by the Enlightenment. He responded to revolutionary terror by emphasising the need to conserve elements of the status quo to ward off social dissolution and violence. While Jean-Jacques Rousseau's *The Social Contract* (1762)[52] and William Godwin's *Enquiry Concerning Political Justice* (1793)[53] take more progressive positions, Thomas Malthus objected to political idealism on the basis of overpopulation in his *An Essay on the Principle of Population* (1798)[54], which helped to shape future utopian debate. For example, in Charlotte Perkins Gilman's *Moving the Mountain* (1911) we learn how that society 'improved the population and lowered the birth-rate at one stroke!'[55]

Political and social movements, such as the Arts and Crafts movement, can also be shown to influence literary utopias. The utopia expanded further in the nineteenth-century as many egalitarian movements appeared; Ricœur lists key leaders and thinkers as 'Saint-Simon, Fourier, Owen, Proudhon'[56]—to which one could add Marx's anarchist rival in the First International, Mikhail Bakunin. They advanced ideas to radically restructure society, imbued with a sense that their dreams were realisable, emboldened by economic, social and technological changes. J. B. S. Haldane's lectures *Daedalus; or, Science and the Future* (1924) exemplify how such techno-optimism eventually reached its partial terminus. Haldane tackles the ways in which we can adapt to technologies and broaches prospects that would inflect later dystopias: 'Moral progress is so difficult I think any developments are to be welcomed which present it as the naked alternative to destruction, no matter how horrible may be the stimulus which is necessary before man will take the moral step in question.'[57] These texts show that at no point does the debate around utopias settle, it evolved and adapted in a way that ignores genre distinctions. And even within, for example the nineteenth-century, the terms of the conversation changed radically. Referring to the British period after 1830, Walter Houghton observed:

> The Utopian dreams of human perfectibility
> which had grown up in the eighteenth-century
> seemed on the point of fulfilment when the
> French Revolution broke out[,] had been
> undermined by the Reign of Terror, the
> dictatorship of Napoleon, the long years of war
> with the succeeding period of depression and
> social unrest, and by the speculations of
> Malthus.[58]

Étienne Cabet's *Voyage to Icaria* (1840)[59] and Edward
Bellamy's *Looking Backward: 2000-1887* (1887)[60] reveal
how utopian literature inspires political movements,
exemplifying the complex boundary between fiction and
theory. Moreover, not only do literary utopias influence
real ones, but also other examples show how real utopias
influenced literary ones; as Deirdre O'Byrne notes about
Marge Piercy's *Woman on the Edge of Time* (1976),[61]
'Piercy's Jewish background surfaces in the many
similarities between the ideals of Mattapoisett and the
original kibbutzim'.[62] In a sense this is arguably present
even as far back as More's *Utopia*, as D. B. Fenlon
contends: '*Utopia* arises from an imaginary fusion of
More's family arrangements and his monastic experience:
the two combine to yield the perfect state—a
commonwealth of cities.'[63] Nathaniel Hawthorne's *The
Blithedale Romance* (1852) shows a similar process
occurring in an anti-utopian novel, where he mocks the
pretences of the real Brook Farm Institute of Agriculture
and Education with his fictional Blithedale:

> "What a pity," I remarked, "that the kitchen, and
> the house-work generally, cannot be left out of
> our system altogether!"[64]

This satirises the idealism of utopian projects, which are

depicted as neglecting the logistics of real world problems. Nonetheless, despite being open to parody, it can be argued that utopianism and utopian literature have a more complementary relationship. Kumar observes of *Utopia* that 'it is never simple dreaming. It always has one foot in reality.'[65]

In any contemporary utopian writings, the broader political context has clear relevance to the genre. Examples of this include the Occupy movement's protests against economic inequality (2011–12), which Noam Chomsky described as an attempt to 'set society on a more humane course.'[66] The tactics deployed by Occupy, such as taking over buildings and implementing targeted protests, had clear utopian meaning. Other potential sites of interest for utopian authors might include Awra Amba, an Ethiopian experiment begun in the 1980s, which has been summarised as 'a unique community [that] has evolved based on egalitarian principles.'[67] In Marinaleda (Andalusia, Spain), Juan Manuel Sánchez Gordillo (who has been town mayor since 1979) formed an intentional community under the ideological melt 'of Christ, Ghandi, Marx, Lenin and Che.'[68] Showing a shift in rhetoric, even the British Conservative Party has switched from its anti-utopian 'There Is No Alternative' (TINA) rhetoric to adopt more prefigurative ideas such as the Big Society,[69] however disingenuously. Additionally there are more utilitarian and technological utopian movements with a less nineteenth-century flavour. For instance, the philosopher David Pearce has formed a community around the idea of the technological abolition of suffering: 'The Hedonistic Imperative outlines how genetic engineering and nanotechnology will abolish suffering in all sentient life.'[70]

Marxism, which is going through a renaissance, is also relevant. Peter Hudis's *Marx's Concept of the Alternative to Capitalism* admits that Marx curtailed the kind of prognostication that is utopia's mainstay, 'reticent about going into too many details about this new society. This is because of his emphasis on the freely-associated character of such a society.'[71] Nonetheless, Hudis rejects the mischaracterisation that there is no normative ideal within Marx's theory and analyses Marx's extant literature to locate a futural vision. His conclusion is that for Marx, reification (*Verdinglichung*), assigning lived existence or qualities like benevolence to an object or abstraction like the nation-state, has real ethical-political dimensions. That is: 'Capitalism is an abstract form of domination that has one over-riding goal: to accumulate value for its own sake. A new society would need to radically reverse this.' There are limitations as 'the future cannot simply be spelled out on the basis of the individual's imagination: it must be traced out through an analysis of existing social formations.' Marx's work is not utopian in Kumar's sense, but neither are Plato or Godwin's. Even so, all that would be required to add to Hudis's account is fictionalisation, and one would arrive at a utopia according to our working definition:

> According to Marx, the amount of time engaged in material production would be drastically reduced in the new society, thanks to technological innovation and the development of the forces of production. At the same time, labour, like all forms of human activity, would become freely associated and not subject to the autonomous power of capital that operates behind the backs of individuals.[72]

Additionally, elements of Marx's ideals can be seen in literary utopias, the fictional, dramatic component of which sets them against reification. This is evidently true in those with direct Marxist inspirations, such as William

Morris's *News from Nowhere*. However, objections to reification can be seen more subtly in, for example, Ursula K. Le Guin's *The Dispossessed* (1974): 'Members of a community, not elements of a collectivity, they were not moved by mass feeling; there were as many emotions there as there were people.'[73] Conversely Philip K. Dick's *The Man in the High Castle* (1962) defines the dystopian Nazi ideology by its excessive capacity for reification:

> Their view; it is cosmic. Not of a man here, a child there, but an abstraction: race, land. Volk. Land. Blut. Ehre. Not of honourable men, but of Ehre itself, honour; the abstract is real, the actual is invisible to them.[74]

Reification is stated bluntly in terms of the abstract being made real.

This wide-ranging discussion of genre and sub-genre reveals the need for a taxonomy of utopian fictions as it relates to dystopia and anti-utopia. Just as utopia (idealistic and serious) is not identical to medieval Cockaygne myths, due to the different solutions proposed for scarcity, as outlined by Davis, anti-utopia (comic and cynical) and dystopia (serious and cynical) must be bifurcated too. These sub-genres have different narrative strategies, that is, resolutions. Whereas the anti-utopias conclude in farce, dystopias end in tragedy. All three genres (utopia, anti-utopia, dystopia) thus can be contrasted. Each sometimes falls under Davis's catchall definition of utopias as rooted in institutional solutions to supply and demand problems, but relate differently to wider debates in terms of tone, style and agendas. The distinction is subtler than between utopias and post-scarcity novels or post-apocalypse fiction, but nonetheless important. Anti-utopias primarily make fun of utopias, while dystopias primarily make horrors of utopias.

Motive is also an important source of distinction within the utopian genre. Two *motives* for writing utopian fiction stand out as dominant and worthy of exploration. David Hume's *Idea of a Perfect Commonwealth* (1754) means to 'inquire what is the most perfect of all' governments, but hopes to avoid a whimsical 'great reformation in the manners of mankind'.[75] Here we see Davis's concern for how societies navigate limits to food, clothing, shelter, morality, human nature. Alternatively, William Morris emphasises subjectivity and self-expression for his utopia *News from Nowhere* (1890): 'The only safe way of reading a Utopia is to consider it the expression of the temperament of its author.'[76] Both novels address conceptions of society and share features: how are resources allocated, power distributed and corruptions averted? Yet for Hume the goal is analytical, embedded in the Enlightenment, whereas with William Morris we see the personal or emotional prioritised over the philosophical. Morris is wedded to a Romantic breakdown of the genre, going back to how 'Schlegel insisted on the singularity of literary texts.'[77] Human intuition and vision become more constitutive of the utopia than generic features such as predictive or formally normative aims.

For many writers of utopias, the motivation is purely aesthetic or unspecific, but Hume and William Morris represent key philosophical and political positions by which we can understand other utopias.

Irrespective of the motive for writing utopias, they are a single genre bound by subjects from economy and reproduction to education and religion. This is demonstrable by juxtaposing two utopias written one hundred and sixty seven years apart. In Huxley's *Island* (1962) the residents of Pala are 'Mahayanists, and our Buddhism is shot through and through with Tantra.' They 'start at sixteen and go on with our education till we're twenty-four—half-time study and half-time work.' Their governance 'is a constitutional monarchy' and 'primitive village communism', while 'Deep Freeze and Artificial Insemination' aids positive eugenics. Such details anticipate criticisms in an attempt to assuage them: 'Pala isn't Eden or the Land of Cockaygne. It's a nice place all right. But it will remain nice only if everybody works and behaves decently.'[78] Alternatively, in William Hodgson's *The Commonwealth of Reason* (1795), established faith is eliminated as 'the greatest scourge that has ever afflicted mankind.' Hodgson prioritises freethinking and learning, 'the most interesting and important of all human objects.' Governance is 'Revolutionary or Rotative' and prevents 'the accumulation of immense wealth' while marriage 'shall be mere responses to repeated dilemmas. Pertinently, More's *Utopia* has been deemed anti-utopian too. Skinner argues that 'almost everything about More's *Utopia* is debatable', but 'his main aim was to challenge his readers at least to consider seriously whether *Utopia* may not represent the best state of a commonwealth.'[79] Conversely, Peter Ackroyd insists that, whereas '*Utopia* has been considered to be a sympathetic narrative that does indeed reflect More's ideal of a commonwealth', in reality, 'nothing could be further from the truth.'[80] They can be contrasted with William Morris who, according to Clive Wilmer, took the book *Utopia* 'very much at face value.'[81] D. B. Fenlon cuts through this debate,, agreeing that *Utopia* is satirical, but arguing that its target is not Christian communism but the realpolitik emerging from religious and political tensions: 'More was exploring the possibility that Christianity and public life might have become mutually exclusive.' And, moreover, *Utopia* must be seen in the context of More's wider body of writings: '*Utopia* argued the impossibility of politics; it was a statement of the case against.'[82] In this reading, More is radically anti-political, rather than defending either the *status quo* or urging a new *status quo*. For Fenlon, More takes a longer-term, patient Christian perspective.

Utopia, then, is a rich and varied genre that is difficult, but not impossible, to tentatively and provisionally contain in useful delimiting definitions. By combining different definitions and understanding what is excluded, it is possible to have a working definition of utopia as a fictionalised account of an ideal society that solves problems of supply and demand through hypothetical social institutions.

Having examined the genre of utopian writing, it is also important to consider its historicity, that is, the wider textual context from which the genre emerged and which shaped it. Doing this will demonstrate that utopia is a genre of literature marked by a conversation between authors' and further show how this genre developed from the early modern period to its current state. My condensed chronology will centre on key transitional texts that reshaped the conversation, such as Harrington's *Oceana*. It will also be complemented by an in-depth comparison between Edward Bellamy's *Looking Backward* and William Morris' *News from Nowhere*. First, however, it is helpful to start with More's *Utopia*.

Navigating between ahistorical heuristics and radical historicisation, both of which risk loosing continuity by bracketing utopia completely or relinquishing the capacity to make generalisations about it, will be crucial to my approach. Fredric Jameson offers a systematic approach that does not allow for generalising from examples to support a coherent thesis: 'For Jameson everything must be historicised; even historicism itself.'[83] When reading utopias, this leads him to see More's *Utopia* outside its historical situatedness, concluding that 'More's own prejudices seem to speak through the text.'[84] For Kumar, however, this kind of reference to prejudice, psychology, etc. can lose sight of the very historical totality that

Jameson, a Hegelian, studies. That is because everything is reduced to an irreducible instance of history, which cannot be compared without losing its historicity. Along with Kumar, I prefer a 'preoccupation with certain characteristic problems and the continuous argument about the best possible solutions to them. All this suggests a tradition.'[85] Historically embedded, tradition and genre can imply both change and meaningful continuity. Both are abstractions, and to some extent arbitrary, but without them it is impossible to find an anchorage in something as potentially broad as the utopian writing.

The Renaissance humanist and martyred saint, More, offers a good point of departure for the utopia within this chronological conversation. As Kumar stresses, More influenced the entire genre, beginning with books such as Tommaso Campanella's *The City of the Sun* (1602)[86] and proceeding to:

> [...] Robert Burton's Anatomy of Melancholy (1621-1638),[87] which has been called 'the first proper utopia written in English'. The seventeenth-century classic not merely critically reviewed the utopias of More, Andrea, Campanella and Bacon; it also presented its own utopia: 'a New Atlantis, a poetical commonwealth of mine own'.[88]

The briefest survey of titles establishes More's impact: it is evident in William Morris's *News from Nowhere*, 'nowhere' constituting the meaning of 'utopia'; Samuel Butler's anti-utopia *Erewhon* (1872),[89] an anagram of 'nowhere', and H. G. Wells's *A Modern Utopia* (1905).[90] Eric Hobsbawm traces More's far-reaching sway so that, by the nineteenth-century, utopia 'became the term used to describe any attempt to sketch the ideal society of the future.'[91] This constitutes a tendency to dilute the meaning of the genre that my analysis resists, as was argued for in the previous section.

In addition to giving the genre its name, More provided its generic content, the aforementioned subjects of economy, reproduction, education and religion. His approach to these subjects has been problematised as the then embryonic conversation between texts grew, and we can see from the genre's beginning serious limitations to utopianism. L. T. Sargent, for example, has uncovered a colonialist attitude, one that represents a repressed continuity within the genre beginning with More and continuing to:

> [...] Theodor Hertzka's Freiland: Ein sociales Zukunftsbild (1890) that envisioned the displacement of the indigenous population to create the utopia[...] And James Burgh's 1764 An Account of the First Settlement, Laws, Form of Government, and Police, of the Cessares, A People of South America concerns the establishment of a Protestant colony in an 'uninhabited' area of South America. Also, Robert Pemberton's 1854 The Happy Colony specifies the creation of a community in an area of New Zealand that was heavily populated by Maori as if there was no one there at all[...] None of these works considered the people living on the land or their displacement as relevant.[94]

Colonialism is an important subject that is addressed in the ustopian genre, which represents the dystopian side of the original utopian dream.

Religion, another fraught subject for modernity, is at stake during the formation of utopia too: 'More's Utopia was closely followed by Johann Eberlin von Günzburg's pamphlet series *Die fünfzehn Bundesgenossen* (1521). Embedded in the series is Eberlin's ideal city state, *Wolfaria*, today acknowledged as the first Protestant utopia.'[93] Leaving the sixteenth-century, the Lutheran *Christianopolis* (1619)[94] by Johann Valentin Andraea and Giovanni Botero's similar *Reason of State* (1589) were influenced by Eberlin's explicitly religious utopias.[95] Utopianism began at the very moment when religion in Europe was destabilised and contested by the emerging Reformation and Counter-Reformation, so More's subject, admittedly secularised by depicting the utopians as pagan, inevitably played into these tensions. Revealing the links between religious and political themes and utopianism, Mark Goldie elucidates how Catholicism:

[…] was not above using Machiavelli's vaunting of Rome's pagan patriotic religion as a model for a portrayal of Christianity as the patriotic religion of the Bishop of Rome's imperium. The genre began with Botero's Reason of State (1589), and was most influential in the writings of Tomasso Campanella. Protestant philosophers turned these claims on their head, or, rather, turned them right side up. The Lutheran Platonist utopias of north Germany, such as J. V. Andraea's Christianopolis (1619), are, in this task of inversion, at one with Harrington's Oceana.[96]

Goldie makes clear that the religious wars and the rise of a new secular politics simultaneously shaped a genre that depicted idealised societies.

It is wrong to posit More as fully circumscribing the genre; new and subordinated contestations fed into this imaginative territory, even if More serves as the progenitor.

In contrast to many utopias, François Rabelais's *Gargantua and Pantagruel* (1534) reconceives the monastic ideal in hedonistic and liberated terms, foreshadowing anarchist and libertarian ideal societies that More did not suggest: 'In their rule was only this clause:/ DO WHAT YOU WILL.'[97]

For Pohl, utopianism during the disruptions of the English Civil War, 'provided a space for women writers.'[98] She cites Mary Cary's, *A New and More Exact Mappe; or, Description of New Jerusalems Glory* (1651),[99] which also anticipates Cavendish's *Blazing World* (1666). The role of feminism in utopianism is examined later as the concerns of women remain largely suppressed in the genre through the sixteenth to eighteenth centuries, with these honourable exceptions.

The outlandishness of Cavendish's travel to another world, via the North Pole, also anticipates soft science fiction and occurs in a context in which fantastical adventures represented another distinct current, a spin-off genre, from More's earthly *Utopia*. This was especially represented in the prolific lunar novels that often have more in common with mythic ideal world stories than utopias, as Pohl suggests:

> Godwin's work influenced John Wilkins to revise his The Discovery of a World in the Moone: or, A Discourse Tending to Prove, That, 'Tis Probable There May Be Another Habitable World in That Planet (1638) and A Discourse Concerning a New World & Another Planet (1640). Both Godwin's and Wilkins's works were imitated in several important ways in Cyrano de Bergerac's Histoire comique contenant les États et Empires de la Lune (1657).[100]

Other unusual utopias written during the seventeenth-century give a sense of the diversity of the period. Francis Bacon's *New Atlantis* (1627) is an example of a scientific utopia involving mastery of the natural world: 'The End of our Foundation is the knowledge of Causes, and secret motions of things; and the enlarging of the bounds of Human Empire, to the effecting of all things possible.'[101] Bacon begins to anticipate the return of the Cockaygne myth in the more contemporary post-scarcity, technological ideal-societies.

With the eighteenth-century rise of the *uchronias* or chronological utopias, we can see how utopia has spanned not just a variety of viewpoints, but also literary forms. In this type, the ideal society occurs in the future, sometimes visited by time travellers from the author's present. However, Daniel Defoe's *Robinson Crusoe*[102] (1719), through its exploration of an alternative society via pseudo-autobiographical confessional fiction and travel narrative, inspired what Sargent dubs the 'Robinsonade', which is closer to the earlier form of utopia.[103] This underscores that this process of change from More's discovered island utopias to *uchronias* was gradual and partial.

The anonymous texts, *The Island of Content* (1709)[104] and *A Description of New Athens* (1720);[105] as well as Robert Paltock's *The Life and Adventures of Peter Wilkins* (1751);[106] and Samuel Johnson's allegorical *Rasselas* (1759)[107] reveal how well-established travel writing and autobiographical conventions became entrenched. Nonetheless, the Enlightenment also developed the Renaissance's emphasis on reason's potential. Vieira therefore traces the literary beginning of chronological utopia to that period, which looked to the future, especially in the context of the (predominantly French) eighteenth-century Enlightenment: 'In 1771, Louis-Sébastien Mercier published the first uchronia (a sub-genre of fictional time periods) *Memoirs of the Year Two Thousand Five Hundred*.[108]

In the Enlightenment context, utopias such as Hodgson's *The Commonwealth of Reason* (1795) imagined human institutions resolving a corrupt clerical past by means of education. Meanwhile, satirists drew on the work of the seventeenth-century English Bishop and humorist Joseph Hall; Pohl observes that *Mundus Alter et Idem*[109] (The Other and the Same World, c.1605) is the first anti-utopia.[110] Kenneth M. Roemer argues that this process of response and counter-response makes utopianism a particularly 'dialogic literature.'[111] Here Roemer invokes Mikhail Bakhtin's term for literature that deploys 'a dialogue between points of view, each with its own concrete language that cannot be translated into the other.'[112] In Voltaire's *Candide, ou l'Optimisme* (1759),[113] for example, the political eschatology of Hodgson et al. is mocked. Sargent claims anti-utopia gave rise to two sub-genres: first, the 'Gulliveriana',[114] which is a word taken from Jonathan Swift's *Gulliver's Travels* (1726)[115] to refer to Aesopian allegories with non-human symbolic parallels, for instance Orwell's *Animal Farm*.[116] Secondly, the 'Erewhonian',[117] derived, as its name also suggests, from *Erewhon*; a genre that relies on reversals, such as a society in which people are blamed for their misfortune and pitied for their immoral choices.

This conversation between texts was not limited to satirists and their anti-utopias, however, but was ongoing between utopias too. The primitive ideal society was a counterpoint to progressive perfectibility, as Pohl notes: 'Utopias such as Denis Vairasse's *History of the Sevarites* (1675) or Gabriel de Foigny's *La Terre Australe connue* (The Southern Land Known) (1676) document simple, virtuous and self-sufficient communities and thus offer their own contribution to the contemporary debate on luxury.'[118] These, in turn, were problematised by the comic tradition. Henry Neville's *The Isle of the Pines* (1668) subverts the later Robinsonade story into obscenity: 'in the year of our being there, all my women were with child by me.'[119] There are, in addition, some more direct examples of nuanced debates between utopians. In 1754 Hume admitted that James Harrington's *The Commonwealth of Oceana* is 'the most valuable model of a commonwealth that has yet been offered to the public', but also outlined its 'chief defects'.[120] As Kumar argues:

> Harrington's ideal republic was astonishingly influential [...] the shape of the constitution of the United States itself, with its two-chamber Congress and powerful Supreme Court, has been attributed to the influence of Oceana though the person of John Adams, a fervent disciple of Harrington's.[121]

In the eighteenth and nineteenth centuries, in the same spirit as Margaret Cavendish's seventeenth-century *The Blazing World*, some utopias remained fantastical, such as the inner-earth and anonymously published *Bruce's Voyage to Naples* (1802),[122] which anticipates Edward Bulwer-Lytton's *The Coming Race* (1871),[123] with its underground, ideal society. Others found unique means to convey their intentions that sometimes invited controversy. In the Marquis de Sade's *Philosophy in the Bedroom* (1795)[124] there is a utopian pamphlet 'Frenchmen, Some More Effort If You Wish To Become Republicans', which for Pierre Klossowski functions as a *reductio ad absurdum* of Republicanism: 'The revolutionary community will then be at bottom secretly but inwardly bound up with the moral dissolution of monarchical society, since it is through this dissolution that the members acquired the force and energy necessary for bloody decisions.'[125] Here we see Sade's ambiguously utopian text operating as a satire cloaked in his political ideals. The work is both a utopia and anti-utopia. Atwood invented the neologism 'ustopia' to characterise the tendency for both genres to be enveloped in one another:

> Ustopia is a word I made up by combining utopia and dystopia—the imagined perfect society and its opposite—because, in my view, each contains a latent version of the other.[126]

Meanwhile, some eighteenth-century texts, such as Thomas Northmore's *Memoirs of Planetes, or a Sketch of the Laws and Manners of Makar* (1795), adhere more closely to the utopian convention in their form, albeit in the service of new, radical politics. Taking inspiration from Aristotle's claim that 'a city is a community of free men', as well as from Newton, Godwin, Christianity and the Stoics, Northmore acknowledges that before creating a new world we must correct 'The great mass of vice and misery which pervade the lower classes.'[127] The utopia itself, which is in a place called Makar, in the city of Macaria, alludes to More by using the name of one of the neighbourly isles from *Utopia*.

By the nineteenth-century utopias in the English language are common. Atwood notes: 'The nineteenth-century, especially the second half of it, was so cluttered with [...utopias] that Gilbert and Sullivan wrote a parody operetta called *Utopia Limited*.'[128] Within this context, Cabet's *Voyage to Icaria* (1842) was inspired by Marx's political philosophy, and served as the inspiration for the author's largely unsuccessful utopian movement. Like William Morris, W. H. Hudson in his *A Crystal Age* (1887)[129] and Ignatius Donnelly in *Caesar's Column* (1890)[130] are examples of writers with an early focus on ecology, whereas William Dean Howells's *A Traveller from Altruria* (1894)[131] is a more conventional celebration of egalitarianism. However, a case study can show that it is Bellamy's *Looking Backward: 2000-1887* (1888), with its sequel *Equality* (1897),[132] and William Morris's Marxist and medievalist *News from Nowhere* (1890), that characterise utopianism in the late nineteenth-century. The tendency is away from Hume's reformism and towards big, ideological projects, the decline of capitalism and liberation of humanity.

Nonetheless, conflict remained in the dialogue. Bellamy's vision was for a technological society where 'the nation [...was] organised as the one great business corporation in which all other corporations were absorbed [...] of which all citizens shared.'[133] This appalled William Morris, who regarded such a plan as prescribing a 'machine-life'[134] and wrote *News from Nowhere* as an alternative, pastoral and libertarian vision.

Of Morris's and Bellamy's books, Bellamy's was both prior and more influential, giving rise to the 'Nationalist' (that is, in favour of nationalisation of the economy) Bellamy Clubs. Yet Morris was also involved in attempts to reshape society, as a Marxist and one of the founders of the Arts and Crafts movement. Both texts are firmly rooted in the ideas of the contemporaneous Left; for Bellamy this means that 'there is no such thing in a civilised society as self-support.'[135] Likewise for Morris, 'it is impossible to see how destruction of privilege can stop short of absolute equality of condition: pure Communism is the logical deduction from the imperfect form of the new society, which is generally differentiated from it as Socialism.' Morris and Bellamy wanted some form of collectivised economics and therefore opposed the prevailing political economics of their day. Both novels are also uchronias, in which a hero—Bellamy's Julian West and Morris's William Guest—travels to the future to visit a changed and improved world. Yet for all these superficial commonalities, the difference between them is not slight and was best articulated by Morris's central complaint against Bellamy:

> [...] the impression which he [Bellamy] produces is that of a huge standing army, tightly drilled, compelled by some mysterious fate to unceasing anxiety for the production of wares to satisfy every caprice, however wasteful and absurd, that may cast up amongst them.[136]

Scale, efficiency and luxury are the virtues of Bellamy's ideal civilisation, 'The principle that makes all operations on a large scale proportionally cheaper than on a small scale.' His is an orderly society in which 'everybody is a part of a system with a distinct place and function.' Moreover, even when permitting private discretion in sexual selection, Bellamy appeals to liberal eugenics as a justification: 'its tendency to preserve and transmit the better types of the race, and let the inferior types drop out, has unhindered operation.' Work is carefully planned; when swapping jobs or moving to another area a worker may do so 'under certain regulations'. All facets of the economy are centrally controlled and managed 'distribution and production supply is geared to demand like an engine to the governor which regulates its speed.'

For the citizens, the benefit of all this efficiency includes material abundance, health, education, early-retirement and a birth-to-death social security system. Moreover, Bellamy stresses the fairness of his model, so that in contrast to the easier work, 'arduous trade, such as mining, has very short hours.' Bellamy also seeks technological innovation, from 'pneumatic transmitters' to the contemporaneously inventive 'credit cards'. For Bellamy, the highest of these accomplishments is aesthetic, as his protagonist West notes:

[...] if we could have devised an arrangement for providing everybody with music in their homes, perfect in quality, unlimited in quantity, suited to every mood, and beginning and ceasing at will, we should have considered the limit of human felicity already attained, and ceased to strive for further improvements.[137]

In contrast to *Looking Backwards*, Morris's *News from Nowhere* eschews regulation and technological flourishes, preferring freedom and a more austere pastoral setting. Bringing together something of the Pre-Raphaelites' medievalism with the Libertarian Marxism of the Communist Left, Morris decried the state socialists. Whereas Bellamy's is a hyper-industrialised world, Morris (contrary to Marx as well) eschews even mechanisation: 'no ingenuity in the invention of machines will be of any real use to us.' Morris's ideas can be traced back through John Ruskin and the early nineteenth-century English textile workers who formed the Luddite movement, protesting against their replacement by machines. Instead, great wealth is created merely by the absence of a parasitical class, meaning that there is 'no compulsion on us to labour for nothing'. Rather, there is a requirement that '*all* work is now pleasurable'. In place of industrialisation, Morris's rich and idiosyncratic aesthetic vision for the landscape and architecture of Britain is given foremost attention:

I need to say a little about the lovely reaches of the river here. I duly noted that absence of cockney villas which the old man had lamented; and I saw with pleasure that my old enemies the 'Gothic' cast-iron bridges had been replaced by handsome oak and stone ones. Also the banks of the forest that we passed through had lost their courtly gamekeeperish trimness, and were as wild and beautiful as need be, though the trees were clearly well seen to.[138]

This textual comparison demonstrates the first of my three theses: that utopia is a genre defined by the conversation between utopian authors such as Bellamy and Morris and that these books are shaped as responses to one another as much as (or more than) they are responses to changes in the broader political world.

The transition from the nineteenth to twentieth-century is registered in utopian writing by another set of concerns and, as mentioned, a move from utopian to dystopian writing as the dominant genre. While bearing in mind the evidence of an earlier dystopic turn, Gregory Claeys claims that 'in the twentieth-century dystopia becomes the predominant expression of the utopian ideal, mirroring the colossal failures of totalitarian collectivism.'[139] W.H. Auden's poem 'Vespers' (1954) sums up this rejection of utopia from a Christian perspective:

> remember our victim (but for him I could forget the blood, but for me he could forget the innocence)
>
> on whose immolation (call him Abel, Remus, whom you will, it is one Sin Offering) arcadias, utopias, our dear old bag of a democracy, are alike founded:
>
> For without a cement of blood (it must be human, it must be innocent) no secular wall will safely stand.[140]

Here we see the view that secular projects to improve the world are inevitably built on human suffering and death, and that utopia is unavoidably corrupted by such sins.

Claeys helps define dystopia as 'portraying feasible

negative visions of social and political development, cast principally in fictional form.'[141] Within the definition we find helpful echoes of the parameters for utopian writing set by both Davis (in terms of the feasibility of the political worlds depicted) and Kumar (with the stress on narrative fiction).

Dystopia is an accretion of anti-utopia. Emerging at the dawn of the twentieth-century with novels such as Yevgeny Zamyatin's *We* (1924)[142] and Jack London's *The Iron Heel* (1908),[143] dystopia has largely (although not entirely) obscured the competing genres of utopia and anti-utopia—although it remains in conversation with both. Will utopian fiction is anticipated as far back or further than Plato's *Republic*, anti-utopianism is prefigured by Aristophanes *The Birds* (BCE 414)[144] and *The Clouds* (BCE 423)[145]. Dystopia has its own conventions, but as we move on to examine the tradition across centuries, it must be noted that, as might be expected from an *intertextual* thesis, the demarcations around genre are rarely perfectly mapped onto the body of literature. Rather, the reality is that there are always cases of texts at the margins that cannot be fully explored here, just as we noted previously with post-apocalyptic novels.

That dystopian and utopian authors continued a dialogue into the twentieth-century explains why utopia and dystopia cannot be simplistically separated. It is therefore important to discuss dystopias.

Just as William Morris wrote his *News from Nowhere* with a critical eye to Bellamy's *Looking Backward*, so too did H. G. Wells' write his *A Modern Utopia* (1905) condemning William Morris, who Wells insists was in error when he decided to 'change the nature of man and things together', a judgement which is reminiscent of Hume's criticism of earlier utopias. Wells cites More, Plato, Howell, Bellamy, Comte, Hertzka, Cabet and Campanella as models for a third way 'between Communistic and Socialistic ideas on the one hand, and Individualism on the other.'[146] During the same period, Gabriel Tarde's *Underground Man* (1905)[147] envisions post-apocalyptic reconstruction shaped by an appreciation of the arts—a very different kind of ideal world. Even as it was receding, utopia looked to a pluralistic literary tradition.

Contemporaneous with Wells and Tarde, Gilman wrote feminist utopias, *Moving the Mountain* (1911), the short story 'Bee Wise' (1913) and novel *Herland* (1915)[148] and finally *With Her in Our Land* (1916). *Herland* remains the most famous of these and, unlike *Moving the Mountain*, moves from the uchronia back to the geographic form that was popular since More. In her preface to *Moving the Mountain*, Gilman shows a willingness to converse with other texts too—Plato, Wells, More and Bellamy—but criticises their 'extreme remoteness, or the introduction of some mysterious outside force.'[149] Arbitrariness and whim are a constant anxiety for utopian authors.

Glimpses of utopia are evident after the twentieth-century dystopian ascendency, often from unusual sources. Austin Tappan Wright contributed the egalitarian and Arcadian novel, *Islandia* (1942).[150] Despite a high-fantasy aesthetic its focus on institutional configurations and fictional realisation roots it firmly within the definitions of utopia offered by Davis and Kumar. B. F. Skinner's *Walden Two* (1948) links to what Kumar has termed 'the modern "eupsychia", the psychological utopias of Wilhelm Reich, Erich Fromm and Herbert Marcuse.'[151] Skinner was intensely aware of the broader utopian tradition, referencing 'the Utopias, from Plato and More and Bacon's *New Atlantis* down to *Looking Backward* and even *Shangri-La!*'[152] Even horror writer H. P. Lovecraft's novella *At the Mountains of Madness* (1931) has the narrator glimpse the utopic civilisation of the menacing

Old Ones in which 'Government was evidently complex and probably socialistic.'[153]

As I am arguing in my second main claim about utopian writing, the twentieth-century produced predominantly dystopian literature, especially after the first two decades. Yet Vieira qualifies this with the observation that 'there was a very brief moment of confidence, at the very end of the 1960s and in the 1970s, which was clearly linked to the student movement of May 1968.'[154] These years of utopian flourishing once again reinforce the conversation between literary and non-literary developments. Sargent gives evidence of these same patterns outside a European context too: 'South Africa has a deeply divided utopian tradition in that most utopian literature well into the twentieth-century depicted the system of racial division or apartheid in positive terms, and after that the same system was depicted almost universally in dystopian terms.'[155] Here we see a general tendency to have utopianism temporarily re-remerge, making any simplistic claims about its disappearance flawed. Peter Fitting contributes to the analysis of utopianism during the twentieth-century by characterising the eighties decline of utopianism within a political-economic backdrop:

> By the mid-1980s this utopian moment [...] had come to an end, however, as that earlier euphoria faded, a casualty of the rise of neo-liberalism (as marked by the elections of Reagan and Thatcher), and by the collapse of the Soviet Union and the socialist alternative a few years later.[156]

The feminist dimension was especially prevalent during the 1970s, particularly in what have been called critical or process utopias; that is, utopias that are incomplete or assumed to be constantly in a state of improvement. It is worth recalling Kumar's definition of perfectibility and noting that some in the field of utopian studies might challenge whether these texts qualify as utopian in the same way as Renaissance examples. The process utopia is not wholly original, for example it is anticipated by Sarah Scott's polemical *Millennium Hall* (1762),[157] which depicts the process of an emerging utopian institution. The tradition flourished towards the end of the nineteenth-century, although Alessa Johns argues that a dynamic, evolving form of utopianism is 'not merely the product of first-, second- and third-wave feminism of the nineteenth, twentieth and twenty-first centuries', but a consistent feature of feminist writing throughout history. Johns outlines and illustrates five features of process utopias that make them suited to feminist goals: education, human malleability, gradualism, appreciating nature's dynamism (ecology) and pragmatism.[158]

Feminist utopias should not, however, be pigeonholed. Elizabeth Burgoyne Corbett's *New Amazonia: A Foretaste of the Future* (1889)[159] is similar to Bellamy's technocratic vision, albeit supplanted to Ireland and with a feminist twist: in both we find state socialism and an oneiric visitation from the present, but in the latter an emphasis on suffragette victory as well as eugenics. Another mode of feminist utopias involves the removal of men, which applies to Mary Bradley Lane's inner earth, eugenicist Aryans of her *Mizora* (1880)[160] and the utopic component of Joanna Russ's *The Female Man* (1975)—taken[161] from different ends of the tradition. Wyndham's short story 'Consider Her Ways' (1956)[162] could be read as a dystopic counterpoint to the all-female utopia, one that makes possible reference to Gilman's *Herland* and, perhaps even more, to her 'Bee Wise', predicated on the titular Proverbs 6:6: 'Go to the ant, thou sluggard, consider her ways and be wise.'[163] Wyndham's book illustrates how the conversation between utopias also extends to dystopias too, which were in turn influenced by other literary traditions as much as political realities. While men exist in Roquia Sakhawat Hussain's *Sultana's Dream* (1905),[164] her novel performs an Erewhonian reversal of gender power to critique patriarchy.

Le Guin's 1966-7 trilogy *Rocannon's World*, *Planet of Exile* and *City of Illusions*[165] started the Hainish Cycle, which includes the genderless society of *The Left Hand of Darkness* (1969),[166] a variation on the all-female approach to utopian society. The cycle also contains an 'Ambiguous Utopia' titled *The Dispossessed*, another book that stresses utopia does not need to be set in a post-scarcity world: 'It's the poverty of Anarres. This planet wasn't meant to support civilisation.'[167] Peter Fitting outlines how Le Guin uses fantastical preconceptions of gender and breakaway egalitarian societies to elucidate 'many of the failings of today's world while pointing to some of the difficulties of the utopian project itself.'[168] A similar claim might be made for many examples of the genre, even going back to More. Piercy's aforementioned *Woman on the Edge of Time* has the protagonist wrongly detained in a hospital, psychically visiting a potential utopian future under threat from another, possibly dystopian future.

Despite the 70s interlude of utopian writing, utopias' general diminishment needs an explanation. Although the horrors of World War and nuclear weapons could be posited as an explanation, this temptation ignores the horrors of previous centuries and fails to explain the seventy's revival. Rather, it is more probable that the accomplishment of many of the aspirations of nineteenth-century Whiggism (suffrage, rotation of power, a free press) as well as the Keynesian post-war Social Democratic consensus made liberal and reformist socialist utopias redundant. In this context the ambitions of a Harrington (such as rotating public offices or broader and more effective institutions of accountability) are moderate. Nonetheless, the post-war consensus collapsed after the 1973 oil crisis, culminating in the monetarists' hegemony in the eighties and nineties. Liberalism has remained strong and no alternative vision of political economy has captured authors' imaginations. This economic account also explains why the process utopias of the seventies represented interests that remained excluded from liberalism's accomplishments, such as the goals of feminists. Percolating through Piercy's novel, for example, are not only the iniquities heaped on gender, but the racial, age, disability, sexual and class injustices within a liberal society: 'Envy, sure, but the sense too of being cheated soured her, and the shame, the shame of being second-class goods.'[169]

Le Guin and Piercy have ecological concerns too, but ecological utopias were also written outside the feminist tradition. Brian Stableford characterises Ernest Callenbach's *Ecotopia* (1975)[170] as making 'the case for an actual technological retreat as the only viable means of averting a dystopian Tragedy of the Commons.'[171] Callenbach's vision is also secessionist, with smaller and smaller states to empower democracy, to such an extent that within his already seceded cluster of some of California and all of Oregon and Washington: 'Jewish, American Indian, and other minorities all contain militants who desire greater autonomy for their peoples.'[172] Like the feminist process utopias, Callenbach's prequel, *Ecotopia Emerging* (1981),[173] published after the seventies, is also a book about an emerging utopia rather than a finished society.

Finding utopias after the seventies generally becomes harder. Kim Stanley Robinson's *The Mars Trilogy* (1992-6) is a rare egalitarian science fiction that stresses pluralism and does not use a post-scarcity conceit, although it posits 'the transformative power of technology over the blank materiality of nature.'[174] Demonstrating the continuing conversation between utopias, Brian Aldiss and Roger Penrose's *White Mars* (2000) can be read as a critical riposte to Robinson: 'Mars must become a UN protectorate, and be treated as a "planet for science", much as the Antarctic has been preserved—at least to a great extent—as unspoilt white wilderness. We are for a WHITE MARS!'[175] Ben Okri's *The Age of Magic* (2014) goes back further, to the pre-utopian Arcadian tradition with its overlapping ideal world themes: 'Arcadia is the place where life is renewed.'[176] It is also possible to perceive utopianism in the titular community of Chuck Palahniuk's *Fight Club* (1996).[177] Commenting on David Fincher's adaptation, Slavoj Žižek observes that 'the message of *Fight Club* is not so much liberating violence but that liberation hurts.'[178] Nonetheless, only rarely or with interpretive gloss are there many discernible examples of utopia in recent fiction.

Some ambiguous late-twentieth-century utopias, however, provide more points of interest. Andrey Platonov's posthumously published novella *Soul* (1999)[179] unites Sufi ideas with the socialist realism of the USSR, but the focus is more on spiritual growth than political organisation. Mario Vargas Llosa's novelisation of The War of Canudos in *The War of the End of the World* (1981),[180] and Toni Morrison's book about an all-black post-fifties town and its relation to an all-female settlement, *Paradise* (1997),[181] share with *Ecotopia Emerging* the notion of ideal communities-in-construction, utopias as non-realised, fragile projects. In Llosa's book, the millenarian Sebastianist-Autonomist group proclaims that 'the time had come to put down roots and build a Temple, which, when the end of the world came, would be what Noah's Ark had been in the beginning.'[182] However, both Llosa and Morrison problematise the fictionalised communities and suggest that they are failures, at least as secular attempts to build a permanent better world on earth. All three books also share historically grounded settings. *The War of the End of the World* and Morrison's *Paradise* feature communities threatened by outside forces. Llosa writes at length on these challenges facing the Sebastianist-Autonomists:

> What matters is what they do. They have done away with property, marriage, social hierarchies; they have refused to accept the authority of the Church and of the State, and wiped out an army company. They have fought against authority, money, uniforms, cassocks.[183]

In this extract from Llosa we see the necessary militarism of the utopians he depicts.

Morrison likewise situates her community in threatening circumstances:

> The whole house felt permeated with a blessed malelessness, like a protected domain, free of hunters but exciting too.[184]

Morrison here shows that the all-female group can only function on its own terms by defending itself from the external peril posed by masculinity.

In contrast with the relative decline of utopias, dystopias are a constant, especially in the later twentieth-century: Bradbury's philistine world of book burning in *Fahrenheit 451* (1953)[185] and more ambiguously William Golding's parabolic *The Lord of the Flies* (1954)[186] are two examples. William F. Nolan and George Clayton Johnson's depiction of involuntary euthanasia in *Logan's Run* (1967)[187] and Philip K. Dick's corporatocratic *Do Androids Dream of Electric Sheep?* (1968)[188] show that dystopia is as keen to narrow its focus on a particular problem (overpopulation, corporate power, etc.) as utopia is to champion a particular cause, such as ecology or women's rights. Anthony Burgess supplies a vision of crime and social conditioning in *A Clockwork Orange* (1962) as well as a strange anti-union homage to Orwell in *1985* (1978)[189]. To this we can add Ira Levin's technocratic collectivist future in *This Perfect Day* (1970),[190] Stephen King's mass-media nightmare in *The Running Man* (1982),[191] Atwood's patriarchal world in *The Handmaid's Tale* (1986)[192] and P. D. James's end of history in *The Children of Men* (1992).[193]

Picking up from the anti-utopian satires, Zamyatin's *We*, which Claeys notes was 'influenced by Wells'[194] as well as Jack London's *The Iron Heel*, set the formula for a frightening society opposed by a hero, to be either crushed (*We*) or ultimately victorious (*The Iron Heel*). Katherine Burdekin's *Swastika Night* (1937)[195] deserves mention too, as it is an early instance of a feminist dystopia akin to Atwood's, as well as providing a vision of Nazi victory like Dick, and strongly anticipating Orwell's motifs of militarism and rewriting history. The most notable and influential dystopias from this period, however, are Huxley's *Brave New World* (1931)[196] and Orwell's *Nineteen Eighty-Four* (1949).[197]

Whereas Orwell focuses on draconianism and punishment, Huxley foresees soft power as the main mechanism of coercion in the future. Wells' *The Sleeper Awakes* offers an earlier middle ground dystopia, where people are controlled by poverty and police, but, showing the same concerns as Huxley, pleasure and hypnotism too: 'Little children of the labouring classes, so soon as they were of sufficient age to be hypnotized, were thus turned into beautiful and punctual machine-minders.'[198]

Huxley also wrote *Island* (1962), another rare example of utopia in the twentieth-century. Claeys insists that 'Huxley was not opposed to intelligent planning for the future.'[199] Nor was Orwell averse to utopian plans; he

45

was a prominent socialist even if he often voiced (sometimes dystopian) criticisms of others on the left. Claeys reminds us that it is important not to caricature dystopians. The most that can be gleaned from their books is that they perceive undesirable potential futures, not that they reject more desirable paths. Still, Kumar makes the observation that anti-utopian sentiment came to characterise theoretical writing too, listing Karl Popper, Leszek Kołakowski and Jacob Talmon as illustrative that 'hostility to utopia has been well nigh unremitting.'[200] To this I could add subtler instances, such as Ricœur's ethical stipulation 'that the utopian imagination always be converted into specific expectations.'[201] However, utopianism simultaneously found many theoretical champions, some of whom will be explored below.

Coming into the twenty-first century, dystopia continued to go from strength to strength as utopia waned, with the phenomenon of the Young Adult dystopian series. Scott Westerfeld's 2005-7 *Uglies Quartet*;[202] Suzanne Collins's 2008-10 *The Hunger Games Trilogy*;[203] James Dashner's 2009-12 *The Maze Runner*[204] tetralogy and Veronica Roth's 2011-13 *Divergent Trilogy*[205] are all dystopias with post-apocalyptic, science fiction themes. Although Westerfeld moves beyond our definition by encompassing post-scarcity motifs too: 'you could use all the resources you wanted, as long as you captured the city's collective imagination.'[206] Other authors continue to write for older readers of dystopias: Brigid Rose's *The City of Lists* (2009),[207] Man Booker Prize winner Kazuo Ishiguro's *Never Let Me Go* (2005),[208] Haruki Murakami's set of three books *1Q84*[209] (2009-10), inspired by *Nineteen Eighty-four*, Howard Jacobson's Man Booker shortlisted *J* (2014)[210] and Jasper Fforde's *Shades of Grey: The Road to High Saffron* (2009).[211]

The relative popularity of the dystopia is relevant to this essay's third thesis: that utopia must engage in a conversation with dystopia to be germane again. Atwood's idea of ustopia (a blending of utopia and dystopia) is useful, but insofar as ustopia has been evident, it is more generally characterised by authors finding dystopia in utopia—and thereby problematising utopia. There are elements of an ustopian uchronia in David Mitchell's *Cloud Atlas* (2004),[212] although this novel more prominently leans towards colonial, romance, noir and apocalypse genres. Based on this feature of his book, it is possible that Mitchell was influenced by the seventies feminist tradition. Le Guin's *The Dispossessed*, Russ's *The Female Man*, Piercy's *Woman on the Edge of Time* and Doris Lessing's 1979-83 *Canopus in Argos: Archives* series[213] also counterpoise utopias and dystopias, but Le Guin also problematises utopia itself by stressing her utopia's material poverty. Even the problem of defending utopia from the outside world in Huxley's *Island* represents only a marginal example of ustopia. Moreover, Suzy McKee Charnas's thematically twinned novels *Walk to the End of the World* (1978) and *Motherlines* (1980)[214] which successively depict dystopia and utopia, does not go all the way to renewing the utopian genre by uniting both traditions at once into a mature ustopia.

Although the dystopia-in-utopia approach to ustopias understands the relevance of dystopia to any attempt to restore the novelistic utopia, it also strengthens a dystopian (conservative, both anti-reform and anti-revolution) suspicion against utopia, i.e. that utopias are all, secretly, dystopias, or destined to be defeated by a stronger dystopian society. A *utopia-in-dystopia*, which is what Mitchel accomplishes, could be argued to encourage a utopian optimism, an attempt to spy utopian possibilities in dystopias.

This survey of utopian (and dystopian) literature does not pretend to comprehensiveness even within its caveats of a tight definition of utopia and a limited Western post-

Reformation period. In addition to books, it is important to note that other narrative media have taken on a utopian aspect. These include films such as Terry Gilliam's *Brazil* (1985),[215] games in the vein of Ken Levine's satire of capitalism *BioShock* (2007),[216] comics such as Alan Moore's pastiche of neoliberalism *V for Vendetta* (1982-89),[217] and television series (in addition to the previously mentioned *Star Trek*) such as Dennis Kelly's Malthusian *Utopia*,[218] which debuted in 2013. Even campaign settings in pen-and-paper role-play games such as Dungeons & Dragons can have utopian or dystopian overtones: 'Founded over a thousand years ago, the kingdom of Cormyr benefits from an enlightened monarchy, hard-working citizens, and an advantageous location.'

Meanwhile, imagining better worlds remains a beguiling preoccupation of modern philosophers. Richard Rorty's postmodern vision of 'liberal utopia' contains citizens who have 'a sense of the contingency of their language of moral deliberation, and thus of their consciences, and thus of their community.'[219] Alasdair MacIntyre's approach is more Aristotelian: 'What matters at this stage is the construction of local forms of community within which civility and the intellectual and moral life can be sustained through the new dark ages.' Consequently he is 'not entirely without grounds for hope.'[220] In Raymond Tallis's defence of the Enlightenment, 'the hope of progress is implicitly Utopian, inasmuch as it is assumed that progress in specific areas will not be at the expense of progress in others.'[221] Suggestions of the genre thus remain in a variety of contexts and ideologies, though it is much diminished.

Writing Nowhere

Writing a utopia is not a formulaic project; many of the best utopias (as I hope my account of its history demonstrates) introduce novel features into the genre. Moreover, as I increasingly believe, the utopia has arguably flourished since the 1970s by diffusing in unique ways into *other* genres—producing hybrid utopian science fiction, utopian travel narratives, even utopian horror.

Nonetheless, there are common features, concerns and considerations. The next mini-essays were written not as comprehensive guides to writing a utopia, but as useful provocations to get you to think about how to go about it. A set of prompts, looking at the where, when, who, what and why of possible literary utopias. If this book inspires one person to write one utopian microfiction, it will have been a success.

Place—imagining nowhere

With that in mind, let us start with the most apparent feature of any nowhere—what kind of *where* is this going to be, precisely?

Places can share many of the same qualities as characters in narrative fiction: they can have backstories and a teleology (or purpose) to guide their futures; an ethos and aesthetic; can change through the story; interact with other places and characters; prove consequential to the sequence of events; have presence in their absence; die or flourish and so on.

However, in the utopia—as in so few other genres—a place assumes something analogous to the role of a main character. That is, the utopia is more often than not the primary *subject* of the story. It can even be titular, as we can find in nowheres such as *Utopia, Wolfaria, Christianopolis, Macaria, Oceana, Olbia, Sevarambi, Sinapia, Mirania, Cessares, Spensonia, Planetes, Icaria, Mizora, Diothas, Amazonia, Freeland, Altruria, Islandia, Triton* and *Gardenia*.

Because of this extraordinary centrality, it can be helpful to begin with some sense of the nowhere you want for your utopia. And the decisions you make here will have ramifications for the rest of the novel. Therefore, it is an area to devote some time to considering.

Even at this stage, you might already have some broader conception of your utopia, its institutions and what you wish to say about the world through your book's conceits. This substantial concept likely embodies the very reason you would want to write in the genre. When More first put pen to paper, it is likely that he had in mind the specific inequities and injustices of his time such as those produced by the enclosures—the theft of common land from the rural poor that was underway during capitalism's birth—and that he had specific things he wished to communicate about this process and its moral and political implications.

That is all for the good, but it can still be helpful at this early juncture to bracket such considerations and instead examine the workings of your world.

Before anything else, you need to depict the setting in which your utopian ideas will be presented. Is nowhere a small and remote island on earth? Is it on a distant planet? Is it deep under the earth? Does it span the globe of some possible future? But even these are just the most preliminary of questions.

Let's say your utopia is an island, as many utopias have been. What kind of island is this nowhere? What are its geographical features? Its flora and fauna? Its climate? And what of its buildings—your utopian architecture, your human habitations. Does it feature metropolises or hamlets or both? If applicable, how does it marry the urban and rural zones?

So early on in this process, we find that we are faced with questions that come to the heart of our utopian concept. And potentially, we are also making choices at this phase that avoid questions other utopias must address by virtue of different choices. For example, an isolated island or a global utopia—be it on earth or a planet in the Alpha Centauri star system—does not necessarily have to explain how its society presently relates to other (perhaps hostile) societies.

If your utopia is a land of abundance, you will not have to address the questions of scarcity thrown up by Ursula K. Le Guin's Anarres. If your utopia is in a peaceful world, you avoid the tragic core of Aldous Huxley's Pala or the Tau in the *Warhammer 40,000* franchise—to pick two utopias with radically different answers to the issues raised by hostile neighbours.

You decide what you want to communicate in your utopia—the scope of its satire, the target of its reforms, the narrative possibilities of its world. But be aware that even as you conceive the landscape—whether this is a mountainous and cold place, or a flat desert paradise—you are already making choices that will delimit and texture your story. Utopia is a genre of profound syntheses—of every element playing into the whole. Play around with one aspect and everything else changes.

For all its importance, deciding how to situate your utopia is not necessarily an arduous process. World creation at this level can be a great opportunity for entertainment in itself. If you have the skills, you could draw pictures of your great glass cities; the interiors of your ideal homes. You could make a map of the galaxy-spanning society of human freedom and flourishing. You can write out descriptions of several key places and go into elaborate detail about the beauty, efficiency and meaning of this or that detail.

If your utopia contains within it religious beliefs, you could make significant and interesting distinctions between how your citizens demarcate sacred and profane spaces. Possibly, this first step will change your ideas and refashion the book you will write in positive ways.

In *A Modern Utopia*, H.G. Wells has his ideal world imagined and reimagined by his opposing deuteragonists on a stage, springing up around them as they break the fourth wall and argue between themselves. Writers from Tommaso Campanella and his *The City of the Sun* to Francis Bacon and his *New Atlantis* invested some imagination into conceiving how someone might experience arriving in their nowhere. Étienne Cabet in *Travels in Icaria* wrote of his visitors first experiences:

> 'At the end of the pier, a gigantic gate, topped by a colossal statue, had the following words inscribed in enormous letters: "The Icarian Nation is brother to all other Nations."'

On arrival, do your travellers experience awe, excitement, or is your nowhere subtler, working its spell on them over a period of time?

The kinds of questions you will encounter as you build your world will continue to preoccupy you as you write your utopia. In the next essay, we will move from the issue of place to the even more expansive one of time—histories and counterfactuals, personal and shared time.

Time—locating nowhen

Time is intimately woven into utopias—every nowhere is also, necessarily, a no*when*. Utopias might be situated in the past (rarely) or (more often) the far future. In fact, the idea of the future comes up in many titles and subtitles for utopian fiction.

We find, then, Anna Bowman Dodd's *The Republic of the Future*, Elizabeth Burgoyne Corbett's *New Amazonia: A Foretaste of the Future*, Albert Chavannes's *The Future Commonwealth*, Kārlis 'Ballod-Atlanticus' Balodis's *The Future State* and H. G. Wells *The Shape of Things to Come*. Time per se features heavily; as in W. H. Hudson's *A Crystal Age* or Alconoan O. Grigsby and Mary P. Lowe's *NEQUA or The Problem of the Ages*. And there is James P. Hogan's fantastically named *Voyage from Yesteryear*.

A utopia might even, as with Nisi Shawl's *Everfair*, find itself situated in radical counterfactual histories—in which, perhaps, the Fabian Society joins abolitionists and a Congolese king to liberate the Congo from Leopold II's reign. Or, a different utopia might be situated in the present, in some distant place rather than removed in time, but nonetheless still saturated by time: with histories that inform their unprecedented accomplishment; that is, the creation of a just society.

Or perhaps they are static, a perfected state in which no change is needed—but even then, coming at the end of history itself (as something that involves change), they necessarily imply strong ideas *about* history and, therefore, also about time. Early Modern utopias are especially redolent of this type.

Many utopias, in a tradition popular in the nineteenth century, begin with fable-like sleeps. Whether literally or allegorically, our travelling heroes are dreaming their peculiar futures. These intuitive introverts seem to discover their nowhens by projecting themselves forward:

both Edward Bellamy's Julian West in *Looking Backward: 2000–1887* and William Morris's William Guest in *News from Nowhere* discover their utopias by this foolproof method. Contemporary parodies of such a style of framing narrative are not uncommon, as we see in Matt Groening's animated sitcom *Futurama*—itself a kind of anti-utopian satire.

Ever since More's foundational text, utopia's have enjoyed their own histories. In *Utopia* itself the founder of the ideal commonwealth, Utopus, conquered the place— which at that point was named Abraxa—and set himself on an apparently successful civilising mission. Many utopias have similarly disturbing pasts, be they colonialist or otherwise genocidal. *News from Nowhere* finds its origins in a great revolutionary upheaval, informed by Morris's experiences as a communist. And Jack London's *The Iron Heel* anticipates fascism as a long prelude to his socialist utopia—a conceit that might be the target of mockery in Margaret Atwood's feminist dystopia *The Handmaid's Tale* and its wry metafictional epilogue.

There is another, subtler level at which time is central to utopias, though; that is, the phenomenology of time. To put it differently: how is time *experienced* in utopia? One common feature, as true for More in 1516 as it was for B. F. Skinner when he wrote *Walden Two* in 1948, is that there will be more time for leisure, which is to say more human time—by which is usually (albeit not always) meant time for some kind of authorially approved self-cultivation.

Morris talks of his utopia as being situated in a period of rest—and there is a definite sense of meditative, reparative ease to the way time flows in his book. It is as if the passage of events were mediated by the now pristine Themes down which Guest travels. This restive quality is not incidental; like all good Marxists, Morris was circumspect about futurology, believing a new political economy would be unimaginably different, radically reconstituting itself according to the parameters of its material conditions. Morris, then, foresees only a period of transition, beyond which we cannot hope to comprehend human social relations.

In Marge Piercy's *Woman on the Edge of Time* we can find yet another version of temporality in utopia—in the fragility of the future. We meet with two possible timelines, utopic and dystopic by turn, in a species of metaphysical conflict in which the present serves as a battlefield. It is hard not to get a sense of Dante about these stakes, and like Dante the drama is ultimately waged over a single soul: Consuelo 'Connie' Ramos.

She is unusual among utopian travellers in that she is neither typically male nor typically white. Rather, occupying an intersection of oppressions, Connie's agency (the very thing stripped from her in the narrative) becomes the focus of utopian (and dystopian) possibilities, which are explicitly temporal possibilities.

As you write your utopia, it would be beneficial not just to decide on your particular nowhen in passing or for convenience sake, but to think more cohesively about how time will mediate your utopia. What are you saying about your utopia, and about the subjects on which your utopia comments?

Learn from the utopias of the past and experiment with time at every possible level. Whether you situate your utopia in a period of transition; between two possible futures; in a counterfactual history; in a static state; with time experienced leisurely or with completely different temporal features, you will communicate much about what you think about the world.

With all apologies for the technical terminology, with history, you must ask yourself deeply philosophical questions: do you have a cyclical view of human events, a dialectal one or a more straightforward eschatological conception of human destiny? Whatever you believe, do not allow such decisions to become the stuff of chance—avoid the pitfall of an unexamined temporality, in which you will be at the whim of equally unexamined metaphysics.

For utopians, time is the very substance of their hope.

Character—meeting nobody

And so we move from the question of when people are living in utopia to the matter of who is going about this business of living—characterisation is a key part of almost any storytelling, but characters can be tricky in utopia.

Characters distinguish the utopia from the ideal commonwealth essay. They breathe life and texture into your writing and, significantly, endow it with a story. Without characters, Thomas More's *Utopia* is little more than an update of Plato's *Republic*. Knowing this, who is likely to show up in this type of story?

Two key types of person appear prominently in utopia, especially as originally conceived: those blissful residents and the curious visitors. Often, the visitor is the point of view, the traveller discovering a strange world—an expositional conceit arguably a little tired in its standard form. The residents are those who not only frame the ideal society—often as guides—but are shaped by it.

How these utopians and visitors behave, their assumptions, present to readers a glimpse into the workings of the world you create. That is, through skilful and nuanced characterisation, you convey the types of subjectivity your world gives rise to. Drawing on the adage of *show, don't tell* (which can be a good guide, but like all such adages should be deployed judiciously), by writing convincing characters you can reveal plenty without the need for long lectures on your nowhere's various and miraculous features—such tedious rants are a pitfall of the utopia that has been inherited by later speculative genres such as science fiction, some horror and a lot of fantasy. In short, good characters are an opportunity to display your society's way of life.

In *Utopia*, More has four named characters: a fictionalised version of the author (such proxies are common); a fictionalised version of More's friend Pieter Gillis; the wholly fictional Raphael Hythlodaeus, who tells of his travels to utopia (and whose last name is Greek for 'expert of nonsense') and the equally fictional Utopus, the historical founder of utopia whom Hythlodaeus briefly mentions. More and Gillis serve to interrogate Hythlodaeus's account and set up the book's concerns, while Utopus represents an ideal ruler (a philosopher king) to complement the ideal commonwealth. The dialogue is the important thing for More, and his characters are constructed to facilitate it.

In his seminal essay, 'Sir Thomas More's Utopia and the language of Renaissance humanism', Quentin Skinner posits a dialectic between More's characters (in keeping with More's debt to Plato), in which his author proxy and Hythlodaeus take different positions on whether a philosopher should involve themselves in the debased business of non-utopian politics. In the same essay, Skinner admits, 'everything about More's *Utopia* is debatable,' which is perhaps expected from a book so engaged in a Socratic dialectic. These characters—reflective of their world—are subtle, and much can be gleamed indirectly. It's an approach that was sadly rare in the utopias to immediately follow More.

Many centuries later, both Morris and Bellamy chose to have their author proxies (William Guest and Julian West) visit utopia more directly, as neither adopts More's dialectic framing. Both books also encounter another popular archetype of the genre: the friendly utopian with free time and a willingness to exposition-dump on the protagonist and point of view character.

Bellamy's affable Doctor Leete and Morris's arguably even more affable Old Hammond go through, without regard to the normal dictates of etiquette, as much about their societies as they can think to tell. This device shows up in some contemporary utopias, too, such as Robert Llewellyn's *News from Gardenia* in which the authorial character Gavin Meckler meets an elderly William and proceeds to be instructed on the ways of nowhere—although here there is a charming wryness and metafictional quality to the whole affair.

Another character becomes apparent in the genre as it grows out of its early modern roots, albeit in such a way as to be easily missed: the sexy utopian. As with any other species of fiction written by predominantly male authors, Laura Mulvey's concept of the male gaze applies. Whether it's the (always) pretty women encountered by Morris's William, or Julian's utopian love interest (conveniently near-identical to his non-utopian fiancée), the women of nowhere usually have varying but deficient degrees of agency—at least until feminist utopias emerged. Instead, women can serve as just another boon of the utopian society—echoing medieval Cockaygne myths about lands of plenty where rivers of wine and self-immolating meat are treated the same way as sexually available women—goods to be freely enjoyed.

Arguably, after More, there were not many substantial innovations on characterisation for a long while—barring Margaret Cavendish's decision to make a woman her traveller in *The Blazing World*, the first (of many) utopias written by a woman. One shift in utopian characterisation did happen, however, with Charlotte Perkins Gilman's 1916 *With Her in Our Land*, the sequel to the better known 1915 feminist (and all-female) *Herland*. Here, rather than a traveller to utopia we meet

Ellador, a traveller *from* utopia. This would be done by Ursula K. Le Guin too, with her protagonist Shevek in the 1974 novel, *The Dispossessed: An Ambiguous Utopia*. As a conceit, it provides a different focus—serving to directly centre satirising the world as it exists rather than getting lost in the minutiae of the world as it might be.

Another innovative way to frame utopia through characterisation is found in Kim Stanley Robinson's *Mars trilogy* (comprised of *Red Mars*, *Green Mars* and *Blue Mars*). These books have a cast of characters to rival any nineteenth century literature, representing different types of ideology and personality such that Robinson creates a tense and diverse conception of utopia, even if one that is broadly committed to radical change. His pluralism encompasses a multi-generational account of nowhere, thereby not only contrasting and comparing ideals, but looking at how generations might reinterpret, outgrow and recover these ideals.

Robinson's blend of family saga and utopia shows that nowhere benefits from the cross pollination of genres. Other examples can be found too. Iain M. Banks's *Culture* series adds space opera dramatics to utopia's usually more toned down conventions; Hermann Hesse's *The Glass Bead Game* uses a utopian setting to enhance the *Bildungsroman* and in a great deal of his short horror fiction. George Daniel Lea suffuses his stories with utopian outcast societies, making fresh starts on the ruins of the old. Such genre mixing allows for a more expansive range of characterisations.

Of all the elements to incorporate into writing a utopia, characterisation presents the most opportunities to innovate. Utopias are full of imaginative nowheres and nowhens, but too often the people of utopia are nobodies in the most literal sense—not ideal, but paper-thin and contrived.

To my mind, Le Guin, Robinson, Banks, Hesse and

Lea in particular point to how to overcome this deficiency and create worthwhile, fleshed-out nobodies to populate their nowheres. After all, what kind of paradise is populated by uninteresting people? It is easy in the abstract to imagine a better model of education, but harder—and more captivating—to concretely imagine the person who benefits from that better model of education.

What kind of person would a utopia mould? Or, to put that differently, what kind of person would a utopia liberate from needing to be moulded? Imagine someone who has cultivated themselves and their relationships without the hinderances and distortions of social inequities. Would utopia be full of sages? Artists driven to confident, unpretentious expression? Can a utopia be a refuge for the unusual and lost? And what differences of personality might endure—flourish, even—in paradise?

Your answers to these questions, as is so often is the case when writing about nowhere, will force you to examine your own philosophical presuppositions about what it is to be a human being. In that lies the great joy of this type of writing, and in this area a rather undervalued joy.

Institutions—governing nowhat

While characterisation can help you demonstrate what a utopia exists to create—a new type of person for a new type of world, there also remains the question of what type of world your characters inhabit—your nowhere's institutions and content.

Institutions distinguish nowheres from the inadequate somewheres utopias critique. You have a place, a time, and characters to populate that time and place. But utopia is a genre about social structures and what these mean for those who operate within them. Even the most allegorical, dreamlike fantasy of plenty must touch on social organisation to some extent to be worthy of the name utopia.

The nowhat that constitutes your nowhere is nothing trivial: it is, depending on applicability within your society's parameters, the governance, economy, defence, culture, education, religion and so on that comprises its substance. It is likely amongst the stuff you thought of first when you decided to write a utopia.

Given how preeminent this subject of content is to the utopia as a genre, you might wonder two things: First, why does nowhat come after nowhere, nowhen and nobody?

Second, but relatedly, why is the discussion of nowhat not subdivided into addressing different areas of this content, looking at the options for economy, education, defence and so on? To answer both questions; there is merit to that different approach, which is why my video essay *How to Write Utopia* adopts it, but there are two other points I have wanted to stress in this series: Firstly, no element of a utopia is divorced from any other; and secondly, the metaphysical assumptions of your utopia (as implied by its handling of place, time and character) delimit and shape the content.

A utopia occupying or preserving an idealised past (see Alan Jaccobs's *Eutopia: The Gnostic Land of Prester John*) is going to have a different relationship to culture than one projected into a sci-fi future (such as Iain M. Banks's *Consider Phlebas*). A utopian travelling to our world will convey different aspects of their nowhere than someone from our world travelling to utopia and back— and deciding which aspects of utopia you wish to convey is fundamental to deciding how you want to dream up the content of a utopia. A utopia on a distant planet with unimaginable, terraforming capabilities will need to demonstrate a different set of institutions than a contemporary one on a small, relatively undefended island.

In essence, only when you have your where, when and who, should you commit more fully to your what. That being said, it is unlikely that you would be so far along without some rudimentary understanding of whether or not your nowhere permits private property, whether or not it has a government and other such issues. What's important to still consider, however, is how do these choices interact? A case study on one of the most basic features of your nowhere illustrates my point.

'They need no lawyers,' writes Francis Godwin in *The Man in the Moone*. A sentiment echoed by the anonymous author of *A Description of New Athens*. Even Thomas More, a lawyer, wrote that utopians 'have no lawyers among them.' Common is the utopia that bans the lawyer—more common than the utopia that echoes Plato's *Republic* by banishing the poet. Rarest of all are utopias such as Ernest Callenbach's *Ecotopia*, which welcome lawyers and embraces a litigious culture. In an ideal society, the temptation is to trivialise law and justice—to assume the workings of your world are above such base things. In any case, you might say, lawyers give rise to corruption and sophistry; concerns for the humanists who birthed the genre.

Whether or not you have a jurisprudence and what type of jurisprudence you elect on, will shape whether or not you have governance (and what type of governance) and whether or not you have police (and what type of police) and whether or not you have prisons (and what type of prisons).

And this question, in turn, will shape how your nowhere chooses to defend itself—or whether it even has ambitions to expand! Questions about professional armies and mercenaries and militias, what each does to shape your society, your economy (if you have one of those) and so on.

Once you reach questions of religion, education and culture, you might find a lot is pre-determined by your earlier choices.

An imperialist, expansionist society with a large traditional army and a hierarchical government (not my idea of utopia!) is unlikely to have a pacifist culture emphasising free expression. Do you have lawyers in your utopia? Yes? Well, then you likely have courts and a judicial system, police and methods of punishment. Watch as your utopia begins to unfold from this one and simple question.

It can be a fun game to take the elements that constitute a utopia in turn and sharply delineate them when setting out your plans. You can create a sort of character sheet for your nowheres. Let's use Étienne Cabet's *Travels in Icaria* as an example:

History: Founded by two revolutionary struggles to overthrow the tyrant Corug and then Queen Cloramide, the exemplary (Utopus-like) Icar assumed power, 'Love of humanity was Icar's ruling passion.'

Government: Based on a set of values (Society, Equality, Family, Fraternity, Reason, Education), power is either delegated rotationally by the people to a Popular Assembly and an Executive Body or retained by the masses in a Republican constitutional and representative democracy. Representatives are chosen from communes. Power is also devolved through a House of Lords (a thousand Communal Assemblies composed of all members) and Provincial Assemblies, which ratify significant laws. This system of referendum is a semi-direct democracy, which is their ideal. Consequently, 'the executive branch is essentially subordinate to the legislative branch.'

Law: There are stringent road safety laws to favour pedestrians; food hygiene is regulated; compulsory quarantines are maintained for some illnesses and a public sleeping curfew is set at 10pm. Serious crime has been abolished by education and communism, which is said to eliminate the passion for murder and the need for theft. Instead, they have minor crimes like tardiness, inexactitude and slander, with minor punishments, which are nonetheless dreaded for the reputational loss. The Popular Assembly acts as the judiciary. Only seduction carries the special penalty of banishment.

And so on...

And in this manner, you can go through the different categories. This can be a useful exercise, but it is important, as you proceed, to think about how each answer is not truly self-contained.

Étienne Cabet's nowhere is not one I would wish to inhabit, but it does follow its own coherent logic—from its foundational (and more admirable) communism to its (less admirable, more naively liberal) governmental structure. This is not to suggest that you ought never to subvert expectations by—for example—having a highly militaristic society that nonetheless, somehow values personal freedom or an anarchist and pacifist one that is extraordinarily rigid about how to live, enforced through a system of public shaming (got to stop the pesky problem of seduction, after all!). But if you subvert expectations, do so deliberately, and therefore deliberatively.

How you build your utopia, how you imagine its institutions, is going to be a large part of what your readers take away from it—get everything else right, and you gain an audience for your imagined ideals.

Motivation—finding your nowhy

The final Writing Nowhere mini-essay asks you to reflect on why you want to write a utopia, the purpose of this place for you as an author and the imagined purposes of your utopians themselves.

Purpose drives all utopias because they seek to overcome the baser justification for society: mere chance survival. To cite Maslow's hierarchy of needs, utopia as a genre might not just presupposes all of the lower needs (how these are resolved can be interesting and instrumental), but it ultimately concerns itself with the fascinating question of what Abraham Maslow dubbed self-actualisation. And, crucially, it concerns itself with this question not at the level of the individual, atomised self, but at the level of the society in which every self is necessarily enmeshed and through which every self is constantly constituted.

But this very presuppositional overcoming of the baser needs opens up a difficult question: what higher justifications can exist for such just societies and worlds? Putting to one side all the ingenious devices, the charming fancies, the celebrations of human flourishing that we expect from these books—to what end do utopias strive, having solved the pettier social questions that still mire real society? Ultimately, then, at the end of utopian imagination, we find ourselves preoccupied with a question that goes under the philosophical category of teleology.

Teleology is the study of ends or purposes—something's telos is its narrative logic, its trajectory. The telos of a utopia is to be read, perhaps to convert the reader to a set of political, social, religious, ethical or mystical ideas or more modestly to challenge them to reassess their current ideas on these topics. The telos of a human being—and, indeed, whether human beings have such a thing as a telos—is a subject of enormous speculation and philosophical controversy. It is also, not incidentally, an idea at the heart of attempts to control people throughout history.

You might think that human beings have a very definite and identified—perhaps God-given—telos (like the Church Fathers and Aristotle); that existence precedes essence and that we must make a telos for ourselves (like Jean-Paul Sartre and the existentialist philosophers) or that human nature is dialectically and historically mediated such that it is impossible to meaningfully divorce from its broader context (like Karl Marx). Or perhaps you have some radically different conclusion. And all of this is before even getting into the trickier problem of defining the content and (ethical, political, economic) implications of that teleology.

Before you get too concerned (or overwhelmed) though, understand that you do not need a philosophy doctorate to write a utopia. These questions should inspire ideas for your fiction, not intimidate you so much that you do not make the attempt to write one. Indeed, once you open up this question, a lot of others follow that can shape not only the characters and content of your nowhere with its nowhens, nobodies and nowhats, but also the broader narrative dilemmas.

For example, it is possible to take this question as a pessimistic provocation by asking: is utopia—not the genre, but the experience or condition of living in one of these nowheres—inherently boring? This is the doubt that plagued Voltaire in the utopian portion of his novel *Candide* (the portion in which his heroes visit El Dorado). In this book, Voltaire proposes that once all our basic needs are met, we find ourselves with no other purpose— the suffering of survival transforms into the suffering of existence itself, a malaise and anxiety so insufferable the pains of hunger and injury are deemed preferable.

If, like me, you are not convinced by Voltaire, it remains to be shown how an existence freed from the basest of sufferings still offers narrative possibilities to us as a species that desire to live within stories, to test ourselves against our limits. Like many utopians (from More, Campanella, Andreae, Bacon, Blake, Morris, Gilman, Huxley, Le Guin, Callenbach, Piercy, Robinson, Llewellyn all the way Shawl in a line from 1516 to 2016) this question causes me to smile and wax lyrical about a whole new basis for our stories: instead of stories of mediocre violences and the oppression of our fellows, we can have stories in which we explore consciousness as an awakening of the universe to itself.

In the great multiplicity of stories we can expect to find in nowhere, we can imagine stories in which art as a domain is effectively abolished by the fact that every person is being artful in every aspect of their lives. In which each and every aspect of life becomes a challenge of aesthetic exploration, which exists simultaneously at the levels of the personal and the collaborative scale of whole societies.

We can imagine a world in which people devote themselves to all the types of relationships (from friendships and romances) available, with a reduced concern for whether or not this or that person has some cynical and exploitative agenda. We can imagine a world in which labour and craft are no longer things callously imposed on those who must perversely sell their lives to live, but becomes how they celebrate their ability to shape the world around them.

If you detect a tendency to become overly abstract here, you are not wrong. If you want to write about violence or starvation or loneliness, we are given many examples in our own world. To write about a world in which everyone is free to live however they wish challenges us to think beyond our experiences and might be impossible to render with absolute fidelity. But it is this very challenge that makes writing nowhere so fascinating.

Realising a utopia in fiction, however imperfectly and imprecisely, is an impressive imaginative act. It requires, at least to some extent, that we set aside an intellectually lazy cynicism and embrace the idea that irrespective of whether we as human beings have a pre-ordained and epistemologically discernible purpose, it is possible that we live better lives than history has so far facilitated.

This ultimately touches on not only why we might write nowhere, but whether to do so is an inherently utopian act and therefore requires no justification? What if the closest we can come to living in a better world, is imaging one? (Put aside the red-herring of perfection, which is not a utopian concern, but perhaps a theological one.)

In 1656 James Harrington wrote *The Commonwealth of Oceana*—we can speculate about what telos, purpose, he assigned the book. Whatever Harrington's ends (likely political), his now little-known work reshaped the world as we know it, such that many people are now living in his utopia (irrespective of whether they regard it as one). As A.L. Morton explains in *The English Utopia*:

> 'John Adams and James Otis, among others in America, were enthusiastic admirers of Harrington's work, and the constitution of Massachusetts embodied so many of his ideas that it was actually formally proposed to change the name of the State to Oceana. The influence of Harrington's ideas can also be seen in the original constitutions of Carolina, Pennsylvania and New Jersey, and it was probably as a disciple of Harrington that Adams insisted so strongly upon a two-chamber Congress for the Union.'

If we understand utopia in a sufficiently broad way, we must conclude that we live in the ruins of the utopias of the past. No author can shape history, but we can take part it in. And writing about nowhere is no bad way to do so. And if you don't, you might end up as a victim to someone else's nowhere.

Beyond Cockaygne

Cockaygne (and The Big Rock Candy Mountain, Pomona and other lands of plenty) are the archetypal folk utopia. Cockaygne is an island of infinite plenty and voluptuous idleness, forever reiterated in the dreams of the worst off. In his *The Last Utopians*, Michael Robertson accurately describes one version of Cockaygne as 'part soft-core pornography[...] and part glutton's dream' as well as an 'effortless, sensual paradise.'

A.L. Morton, in *The English Utopia*, adds that 'it is a land of peace, happiness and social justice'; one that bars the underserving rich from enjoying its goods. Morton sees in folk utopia, as well as an answer to the surfs' neglected needs, 'a foreshadowing of Humanism, the philosophy of the bourgeois revolution.' And Morton singles out William Morris's *News from Nowhere* as the highest development of utopia, unifying Cockaygne's pleasures with the ideas of the intermediary philosophical utopias.

Robertson—who also has a lot of time for Morris—sees Cockaygne as foreshadowing something else too; citing philosopher Louis Marin, he evokes the degenerate utopias of Disneyland and cruise ships, 'fantasies of escape, with one foot planted in Cokaygne, the medieval dreamland of leisure and effortless abundance, and the other firmly planted in contemporary consumer culture.'

The comparison between utopia and cruise ships can be found elsewhere. For example, in Marshall Brain's 2003 utopia *Manna: Two Visions of Humanity's Future*, where a utopian Australia of infinite plenty (facilitated by recycling, machines and AI) is described as like 'living on a gigantic, luxury cruise ship. The trip is already paid for, for life, and you are free to do whatever you like with your time.'

The desire for idleness and pleasure is strong in utopia.

Although most utopias, including Thomas More's Utopia, are not at all Cockaygne—emphasising self-cultivation and cooperative work over pleasure and idleness—it is Ursula K. Le Guin's 1974 *The Dispossessed* that most subverts the utopia as Cockaygne trope. Her Anarres is on another planet, in the complex universe of her Hainish Cycle (many books of which are neglected masterpieces of science fiction).

Anarres is a planet of extreme scarcity. It is no cruise ship, but its anarcho-syndicalist philosophy affords other gifts: the freedom not from work but from alienated work, the abolition of oppressions. By locating paradise in a would-be hell, Le Guin arguably (however ambiguously, as Anarres is ambiguous) demonstrates a profound optimism. And perhaps a profounder rebuke to the later logic of Margaret Thatcher's TINA (There Is No Alternative).

Moreover, Brain's *Australia* might offer plentitude, but its hero Jacob Lewis elects to forgo many of its pleasures and live in a commune recreation of Williamsburg, adopting a way of life more like the communists of William Morris's ideal future than the tourists populating a pleasure cruise. He describes how his commune 'worked together to build their own houses, grow their own food, make their own clothes, practice simple crafts and trade with one another.'

Even Brain's narrator is a little surprised at the decision, 'with all this technology available, I choose to live my life by setting time back 300 years and living a very simple, completely physical lifestyle.' Ultimately, the plentitude of this utopia resolves a different problem than a lack of sumptuous pleasure—i.e. how to live happily while knowing others are not. Once inequity is done away with, Jacob Lewis requires only the simplest existence, free from the risk of illness or destitution. Tamed pleasure is the thing.

As a genre, utopia confronts the most intimate aspect of human imagination: the limits of our desire. Cockaygne articulates our essential needs, while utopias by authors such as Brain and Le Guin go beyond that baseline and arrive at different (even if sometimes comparable) conclusions.

Few other genres focus so directly on this most frightening question: what, precisely, do we want? Here is an opportunity for any author to write in such a way as to show the greatest poverty or richness of their imaginative landscape. To expose themselves completely, if we are to accept Morris's brave assessment that:

> The only safe way of reading a Utopia is to consider it the expression of the temperament of its author.

In Epicurus's necessary delimiting of hedonism; William Blake's *The Marriage of Heaven and Hell*; the Cenobite monsters in Clive Barker's *The Hellbound Heart*; Jacques Lacan's notion of a *jouissance* that goes beyond the pleasure principle; Georges Bataille's handling of transgression and evil; the demonic God Slaanesh in the Warhammer 40,000 miniature war-game, we meet again and again (in philosophy, poetry, horror fiction, psychoanalysis, literary theory, pulp myth) a provocative dialectic that provides the absolute subversion of Cockaygne's presupposition.

What if pleasure and pain fold into one another? What if the greatest excesses of one becomes the other; as in the I Ching when Old Yin becomes Young Yang and vice versa. And what if heaven and hell are not distinct, as in Dante's *Divine Comedy*, but wed? Perhaps this intuition explains why Brain and Le Guin do not make their utopias primarily about pleasure. Does this metaphysic preclude paradise? Or make of it something weirder (and more perverse)?

I would not pretend to have answers to those questions. I doubt that there are definitive answers. Rather, in writing utopia, there is the mere possibility of a new working out of such dilemmas. And that is why it is such a vital genre to keep alive.

The questions of utopia are not addressed properly elsewhere. Alone, dystopia serves only to erect austere walls around the scope of our thought. And rather than being a transgressive genre of social critique, what if—especially as an alternative to the utopia—it merely protects us from addressing the transgression inherent to utopia? The transgression of facing up to social desire?

You are a traveller at sea (under the sea, in space, through dimensions or time, underground), and arrive on the distant island (place, plane, planet) of Cockaygne. At once, everything is possible. And not just for you—you are no atomised Robinson Crusoe—but for everyone within the scope of a whole and living society.

But everything Cockaygne permits is still without content. Into that fearsome void of potential pleasure, what can you imagine? To echo Immanuel Kant's Enlightenment challenge, do you even dare?

Letters from Nowhere

This short story first appeared in *Citizens of Nowhere:
a Utopian Anthology*, where I described it as 'as much
a commentary on utopia as a narrative belonging to
it.'

Every time I pass the furniture shop down the main
street in town I look inside the third window along,
which contains a tableau taken from the life of
some fictional person, the woman—or man, I guess—who
is supposed to have configured this desk and bookshelf
arrangement: its leather bound volumes of the kind few
people now own, and an old-fashioned map draped over
the writing surface in all its poised clutter.

These are cues that are all chosen to suggest the life
that the intended buyer should wish to live. I want another
life, too; I want to be entirely somebody else and
somewhere wholly other.

The nondescript cream envelopes were unstamped and
unaddressed. They arrived at night, I think. Once I stayed
up with Bernard dozing on my lap, flitting in and out of
consciousness beside me. No letter arrived. At five in the
morning, Bernard woke and barked, unusual for the old
dear.

The regular mail only included a gas bill and a fifty
per cent off coupon for the new pizza place in town. A
letter from nowhere—that was how I would come to

describe them, thanks to Sayer—had not arrived through the mailbox, but when I went into the bedroom one of those envelopes was waiting on my bedside table next to the Tiffany lamp that Samantha bought me; that was where I would often put letters before reading them. It had materialised, as if from the ether.

The next day, the letter arrived as normal, sitting beneath the spam and official correspondence that the regular mailman dutifully delivered. It was like all the other letters from nowhere, including the one I had discovered on my bedside table. It started and ended the same as every other had.

Dear Carol,

...

Your doppelgänger from nowhere,
Carol

The sender wrote at length and created in her writings what I then thought to be an elaborate falsehood. And in her fantasy, she and I were almost the same person, but whereas I inhabited a small bungalow and felt so completely alone, she inhabited this other world—the one I found so tempting, the one I craved. Most of her writings were about some fictitious nowhere that she had contrived and traced in detail: the geography, governance, economy and architecture. She was exhaustive and meticulous and sometimes tedious.

In her fantasy, the period she called 'reified human history' ended two and a half centuries ago, and this history corresponded closely enough, if not exactly, to our actual history up to around the year 1800. For over fifty days she expounded on eleventh century England, which she says is her speciality as a 'historian of the reified human.' Much of her exposition corresponded with what I read elsewhere at the time, checking her facts against those of agreed history.

After the end of rarified human history, my doppelgänger from nowhere told me that there was a painful birth of a society rooted in the joys of what she called free labour. Humanity had been renewed and true human history begun. Humanity, she stressed with the repetitiveness of a religious mantra, had until then been alienated from itself. She gave numerous historical examples of such alienation from mass violence to awful working conditions. She had an almost monomaniacal obsession with the worst cruelties and would describe everything from the minutiae of tortures to the horrific deprivations.

> For those hanged, drawn and quartered, the victim would be bound to a wooden panel, delivered by horse to the stage for the dreadful act. They were hanged, but not allowed to die of a merciful affixation. That way they could also have their external sexual organs removed—it was punishment reserved for men, whereas women would be merely immolated. They would also be disembowelled, beheaded and finally, literally, quartered; that is, chopped into four pieces.

Nor were her descriptions reserved for the distant past. Narrating a more contemporary war, she documented the lives of captives.

> The smearing of human excrements on detainees' bodies was not an uncommon practise. The shit would be pasted across their skin, left to mangle and matt with their body

hair. It was either believed that valuable military Intel could be gleamed from the humiliation, or, more likely, it was a method of relieving the abusers' stress and channelling their complex moral and psychological traumas.

Everything in her fantasy, an alternative to the macabre portrait of our world, began from a different footing than it would in our reality. Education, childrearing, religion, work, culture, violence, law—it required, this other Carol enlarged, a way of thinking that would be alien to me. She would stress that in terms I found utterly, exhaustingly patronising.

I did not read every letter. In the early days, when I hoped they would stop and feared their daily arrival, it was my revenge to miss a series of them. They would appear and disappear every day. They could not be kept.

Nor could they be shown. Any attempt resulted in their prompt disappearance. I would leave them somewhere definite, on a table, tacked to the fridge, within my safety box, but they would be gone all the same. I would watch them through the whole of a night, and while the thick paper would remain, it would be blank. I would look at the words through the whole of the night, but at some point I would blink and, just as surely, the words would blink out of existence too. They existed only for me. And I assumed, were a product of my febrile mind. What I came to learn later does not clarify anything. I'm writing this only because it helps me to process what has happened, not because it helps me to understand.

It was a Sunday morning and I was having difficulty with the pain. I swallowed the eighteen pills, more than half of which were medication to counteract the symptoms of the other medication, a few of which were even medication to counteract the symptoms of the medication that counteracted the symptoms of the medication. I was the old lady who swallowed the fly—I would, and still will, die.

I took the pills with the coffee the beautiful Samantha—with her pixie cut of lush brown hair and her generous smile—made me every morning. She would arrive at eight, have my coffee and porridge to me by nine and then take Bernard for a walk; the old beagle did not need a long walk. At half-ten, she would check on me one last time and leave. On Sunday mornings my son, Joseph, joined my community-obsessed daughter-in-law. The puffy rings around his eyes growing more and more so that he reminded me of a panda bear.

This was often all the human contact I had for months. Bernard helped to keep me sane. And the letters, however disturbing, did at least break the monotony. I resisted television, radio and the Internet. Those passive entertainments felt like a surrender. I could no longer manage to read a long novel. I struggled to keep up with the stories. The letters, though, catered to my condition.

Back then, on good days, I could still potter about outside. And in the front garden I had a bench were I sat and read the other Carol's missives when their content did not upset or bore me, and I chose to engage rather than ignore her horrors or tedious lectures.

If I had been younger—and healthier—curiosity would have propelled me sooner to research. Not only to investigate the content and claims of the correspondence, but the simple and impossible fact of magically appearing, magically disappearing, post. But I was neither. I could experience days without coherence, where thoughts would bleed into one another and the discomfort of wakefulness slid in and out of my delirious sleep. Grasping the reality of something so irreal, and doing so long enough to sustain curiosity, was a feat I only accomplished after seven months of receiving the letters.

At that time, I checked my emails about once a week

on the old machine. I would wait for it to boot up, beeping, as I sat at my bedroom desk, placed against a window looking out across the various striking blues, yellows and reds of my garden flowers. The machine would always crash onto a blue screen, what Joseph called the blue screen of death, and I would turn it off and turn it on again and it would start-up properly, if still laboriously. Then I'd open my inbox. I let the emails download for half-an-hour and returned to it to delete almost every one. Occasionally, there was a message from Joseph or the NHS, but most of it was for penis enlargers, Russian blondes and diet pills. And as I had no penis, had long lost interest in blondes— Georgian or otherwise—and could use more weight not less, all of it was for nought.

I had not touched the browser for over a year, having once been an obsessive addict of the online world, a hypochondriac and devourer of medical factoids, attempting to become a specialist in my own symptomatology. Charting every ache, every pain, offering my own prognoses, I competed with the pessimism of my doctors, conceiving worse and worse fates for myself. But eventually, after finding some gruesome pictures of my affliction untreated, I cured myself of my obsession and quit the web. But it was still there, my Mozilla Firefox— the delightfully named browser by which I entered this disembodied world. And there was a letter from Carol on the computer desk, one I had been reading all morning. It told me about Carol's upbringing, how she moved from family to family at will, how she had met her best friend and sometimes lover Sayer Kilby Bailly.

I typed the name into Google; if more than one Carol Vaughan existed, why not another, but real-world, parallel for Mr. Sayer Kilby Bailly? Someone who, in that other world, had grown up alongside my doppelgänger, but in this one had never met me. It demonstrates just how far gone I was to be thinking according to the logic of these letters, but I did not truly expect to find anything. And I definitely did not expect to find Dr. Sayer Kilby Bailly.

Not only did he exist, but he had a website called Letters From Nowhere dedicated to the mysterious snail mail.

He wrote, 'These letters are far too consistent and are received by people considerably too removed to be a set of unique delusions the similarities of which are explainable in terms of cultural tropes. Perhaps some semi-mystical mechanism such as the Jungian collective unconscious provides an explanation, but whatever the reason for them, I am utterly persuaded that the majority of people who receive letters from nowhere have no shared basis for their claims.

'Nonetheless, they do share a common trait. If you have found this website because you are one of the recipients, be forewarned that you may wish to stop reading at this point. I do not wish to bring you any distress. What I am about to convey might be something you do not wish to read.

'They all, without exception, die a few years (generally around two to three) after receiving their first letter and about two months after they receive their last letter.'

I stopped reading.

My first letter had arrived just over two a half years ago. If Dr. Sayer Kilby Bailly was right, I had less than a year left. And reading those words took me back half a decade to the dull, sterile white office with its slatted curtains looking out to a concrete car park, and to the long-faced, greying doctor who delivered my less definite but still wounding prognosis in a dulcet tone.

I learned a long time ago to take a practical approach to time. My body aches and if I stare into the middle distance hours vanish. At first this aspect of my illness was a locus of resentment; not only was the sickness shortening my life—fifty-four and I am like an invalid—but it was robbing even the lucidity I possess for the time I have remaining. My time was being stolen from every direction: my past taken in the form of memories, my present, in my inability to hold on to waking, active life and my future by my imminent mortality.

But to resent time is just too heavy a resentment. So, gradually, I took an easier approach, happy for every daily allotment of success—just getting out of bed, a shower—and unconcerned by the inevitable, and inevitably more common, failures. When it came to time, I held the lowest possible expectations.

It was a fortnight before I returned to Dr. Sayer Kilby Bailly's website. But as I experienced that passage of moments, it could have been later the same day or after the elapsing of a whole year.

I wrote him an email outlining my situation.

He emailed back the same day, although I saw and read his email three days later:

Dear Ms. Carol Vaughan,

I hope this email finds you okay. I am so sorry to read of your illness and distress.

And I am sorry if my website in any way contributed to the latter. I have the utmost belief in your letters. Your approach of keeping them secret is not rare. So much so that I wonder how many recipients never convey the important missives delivered to them and how much knowledge of this other world is consequently lost.

Your scepticism is understandable, but I assure you that your letters are real. That the other Carol exists and, I strongly believe, communicates to you from benign intentions only.

Please, if I could visit you anywhere, at any time of your choosing, I would deeply appreciate a chance to talk in person. Especially since you are the first person I have met who claims that my name was mentioned in a letter. Perhaps one day this other Sayer will write to me too?

Yours sincerely,
Sayer

It was another four days before I decided to reply and a further three to fully draft and edit my response:

Dear Sayer,

Thank you for your email. As you know, I am not well, but I am prepared to accept a visit from you after my son and daughter-in-law have left from their weekly visit, at 1 pm this next Sunday. Please, do not expect too much and be prepared for a very short visit.

I want to know more. Please find my details below.

Warm regards,
Carol

Small, elegant rituals still gave my life dignity. And one of my favourites—along with preparing espressos and sitting down to read—is using a letter opener. I used it on every letter from nowhere. And when Dr. Sayer Kilby Bailly's first class letter arrived with the day's letter from nowhere, I happily used it on that too—charmed that he had opted to reply offline. His letter was short:

Dear Carol,

I will arrive at the date and time given. I look forward to discussing your letters.

Yours sincerely,
Sayer

That Sunday my son's visit dragged. My eye looked to the dark grandfather clock that ticked behind Samantha and my Joseph. As usual, Joseph was quiet, staring out of the dining room window into my garden where he had played on the lawn as a boy. He was looking at the sycamore tree still growing there. Samantha talked about her work at the accountancy, weather, documentaries she liked about history or geography, the local branch of the Liberal Democrat Party and redevelopment in the town centre. Neither one of them looked at or spoke to one another.

They left at 12.30 after Samantha cleaned up and I waited another forty-seven minutes before the doorbell rang. He smiled awkwardly as I let him in, and slouched at a bit too much. It took him a while to get going, but when he did the initially taciturn impression he gave was completely dispelled.

'One of those contacted, he received vivid descriptions of the cities,' continued Dr. Sayer at getting close to midnight that day. He was a short, balding man whose rotund face was framed by a closely cut red beard and large, flappy ears. He had a shy grin that belied a manic comportment when he talked of matters relating to the letters. I loved his energy. 'He did not save the writing, but was an illustrator for a major publisher. So he drew the descriptions from his letters from nowhere. These are a rare glimpse of this other place. He gave them to me before he died; he said that nobody else would appreciate their significance. I present to you, Carol, the closest we have to photographs of this utopia.'

The beige portfolio he put down on the pale wood of my living room coffee table opened up and out spilled charcoal drawings of buildings. They were like the brutalist buildings of postwar London, except larger, more monolithic and even more ambitious in their elaborate shapes and sizes.

And there was a cleverer use of plants than I had ever

seen in any real city. The monochromatic grey of the sketch at first disguised the verdant use of shrubbery, but soon I perceived that between the buildings was a thick veil of trees, and every window sported more florae so that it was as if the buildings were repositories for them rather than people. It was a city, but overgrown, a forested metropolis of strong slab monuments.

I wasn't sure what to say as he smiled from the settee, but his use of the word utopia had irked me. 'I don't know if I would call it a utopia,' I complained. 'This other Carol is insufferable and sometimes even a little frenzied. She is always condescending, especially when writing about the history of her world and in her presumptions about ours, and about me; she is a snob. If such a person is a product of utopia, perhaps I am glad not to be.'

He kept smiling. 'I met a young man fifteen years ago, one of the first to get these letters as much as I can tell, and he told me the same thing; although, I didn't call them utopian then. Now I'm convinced. Although they are not flawless angels, their world is a kind of paradise.'

'Uh-huh,' I murmured.

'Here, look at this one,' and he shuffled through the pile of pictures to one depicting a pathway through a forest, but with buildings rising up beyond the canopy. The artist had rendered dappled light and depicted a huge crowd of people in some kind of parade, in various costumes: great, flowing dresses adorned men and women, billowing back like ship sails; elaborate hats with points and orbs and more fluttering fabrics; people in close fitting garments with patchwork designs like troupes of harlequins; masques depicting great grotesques smiling and laughing and grimacing.

'Carol always made me think of them as austere. I had in mind a society of intellectual idiots.'

'If there is one thing I have learned in my time studying the letters from nowhere, it's that utopia is a diverse place. It has an abundance of everything, a multitude of ethics and faiths and so many ways to live. Until you can interpolate more than one set of letters people always have the impression of a world taken to a single monomania. This artist believed it was a carnival utopia, a world in constant celebration. He believed that because that was his doppelgänger's life. Your Carol is, perhaps, something like an academic, maybe a member of some society of readers or perhaps a hermit contented with her studies.'

'There are hermits in utopia?'

'Apparently. This world, this other world, permits so much more variation than ours. As far as I can tell, it reviles any attempt to impose a single template on life.'

I nodded and sipped my now cold tea. I was suspicious of all of this. I imagined coming to some vile dystopia and watching an agitprop film, like the ones doubtless made by the Nazis, describing the glorious accomplishments and perfect lives of the citizenry. I was also tired. My legs hurt and there was an uncomfortable, bloated feeling creeping from my belly to by chest, which made me irritated at having a guest present.

'I… it was…'

'Ah,' he held up his wrist, checking a clunky watch, 'I have overstayed.'

'No, not at all.'

'But I have. And I should be making my departure.' He smiled, showing off some crooked but clean teeth. 'Can I come back?'

'I…'

'You don't have to answer right now.'

'Yes, you can. Come the Sunday after next if you wish.'

Dr. Sayer Kilby Bailly is not the kind of man I would have been interested in during my youth. He was silly, excitable, a bit myopic. But weeks of enforced isolation made me happy for his attentions, even if he was mad.

When I told Samantha about him she was very interested, 'I will Google stalk him for you,' she said.

'Stalk him?'

'It's normal and it's only online, you know, to find out if people are okay. I always look them up to make sure they're not part of a cult or something.'

I agreed, reluctantly.

The Saturday before he was due to visit the second time, Samantha came to me with a deluge of information. She took Bernard off his leash and watched as he huffed over to the couch to take a long afternoon nap, snoring loudly.

'This Sayer guy part-owns an antique bookshop in London, Tomorrow's Novel. I think he runs it with his brother. They inherited the business from their father and it's famous. Been around for decades and in the same family. He has a few nieces and a dead nephew, but I don't think he's married. His PhD is in biochemistry, but there's no evidence he's ever really used it. And he runs that website you mentioned. It seems kinda big. Like, there's a Facebook group, a hashtag on twitter...'

'A hashtag?'

'It's like a key word that you can use on the social network.'

'Like Facebook?'

'Yeah, kinda. Anyway, these letters from nowhere are all over. Hey, Carol, is that why you see him? Do you get these letters?' She looked at me with her mouth clenched. She breathed in sharply.

'Yes, but please don't tell Joseph.'

Samantha laughed, but as though she hadn't meant to laugh so that it was a little violent and quickly repressed. 'Sorry, no... I mean, we don't talk much. I think the world of your son, y'know? But...'

'It's okay,' I interrupted.

As with his previous visit, Sayer was excited to talk about his favourite subject. He started, with little encouragement, by defining what makes a utopia a utopia. 'I think J. C. Davis, Karl Mannheim and Krishan Kumar provide the best definitions,' he said, as if I knew any of those people. 'They don't all agree, but we get a good idea by taking aspects of all three. First,' he held up a stubby finger, 'we need to distinguish, as Davis does, between a utopia and other ideal-worlds. For example, a utopia is not like the island of Cockaygne…'

'The island of Cockaygne?'

'Yes, it's a medieval Irish mythical place where sailors occasionally wash up. It has shops that give everything away for free and rivers and houses and streets made of infinitely replenished food. Birds will fly out of the sky and land compliantly on your fire to roast themselves for your pleasure. There's a more futuristic term for this kind of place, a post-scarcity society. A lot of modern science fictions use inexplicable technology to create the same result, but a utopia is not a world without limits. It's the world, as it exists, populated by people as they are, but it's better organised. The institutions are what makes it different.'

'Okay,' I said.

'Next,' Sayer held out two fingers, 'we need to understand that utopia is not about perfection. It's not perfect institutions, no more than any utopian author can expect to be able to devise such, but just better, according to someone. Mannheim gives us this part. And finally,' he held up three fingers, smiling, 'Kumar says that a literary utopia is always conveyed in a story. I think the letters from nowhere, therefore, count as utopian. In the literary sense, even if, perhaps, in some other way, they are not wholly fiction.'

'I wonder why they communicate by letter,' I mused out loud, hoping to break his flow a little.

'It is not always just letters,' he answered quickly. 'Sometimes it's emails. Especially when it involves younger people. And for one person I met, it was phone calls. Everyday a phone call, by mobile.'

'You mean, someone talked to one of these doppelgängers?'

'No, it was a pre-recorded message. And the voice was robotic, like a computer reading out text. At least according to the women who received the calls, I never heard any of them, just as I have never seen a letter from nowhere. Nobody, as far I have been able to discover, has ever talked back to nowhere. Utopia has somehow found a way to talk to us, but it has never been the other way around.'

Sayer reminded me of my other self's way of talking, of the other Carol's sometimes endearing pomposity. I always got the impression that he loved his own voice, was intoxicated by his own words. Not in a bad way, although he could be smug, but as if he was bewitched with wonderment for any subject on which his mind rested.

He would talk on tangents on and on, his voice merging with the ambiance of my home—the dulled whoosh of cars from outside, the chirping birds from the garden, the whirr of my fan during a suffocating summer day.

There would be a lull as we drank tea, sometimes I would even drift off. 'As far as I can tell,' he would start, apropos of nothing, looking up from a pile of papers, 'they have something akin to a celebrity culture, but their celebrity culture is very niche. In fact, this quality of niche is what prevents them from being aristocratic, really. It's what holds in check their social resentment, which the evenness of their distribution would otherwise leave out of control.

'They have no household celebrities for the simple reason that they have no pervasive household culture at all. Instead, their society is a great, shifting, overlapping sea of parochialisms, adapting and altering too fast to be documented or understood holistically.

'Certain people are famous to a subset of aesthetic devotees, which will change depending on the given artist's—and they are all artists, in some sense—style of the moment. And every artist will in turn be a devotee. It is a utopia of writer's writers, painter's painters, architect's architects.' In this way he would continue and could do so, uninterrupted, for as many as five or six hours before becoming flustered, apologising, asking if I still wanted him to visit, and arranging to come by the next week or—if I felt very tired—the week after that.

Waiting for Sayer's visits had a peculiar benefit. It slowed down time. He was sometimes insufferable, but always entertaining, and because I wanted his company I felt the weight of time between each new encounter. Sayer had restored something to me, however accidentally, and I felt the same kind of gratitude to him as I had previously felt only to Samantha.

I wondered a lot about Samantha and her devotions to her husband's mother, despite her failing marriage. What obligation compelled her? I would have tried to free her of it all: myself, my son. Nobody should waste away in a loveless marriage. But I was too scared by the material implications. I selfishly wanted to keep her. And not only as a visitor, not even just as a dog walker. Seeing them—the loveless couple—sitting with each other every Sunday morning, would make me horrendously guilty, the kind of guilt you feel physically, a nausea.

I found myself asking, what would the other Carol do? No doubt sniff haughtily and accuse me of the kind of behaviour she loved to call alienated, a descriptor that she would apply equally to the crimes of hiring someone at a low wage and flaying them alive before a mass audience. Still, I wished I could ask her, ask my better self, I suppose.

The question that always hurt me most about the letters from nowhere, the questions that hurt so much it was more than ten visits before I could ask Sayer his opinion, was 'why is she not sick?' These people from nowhere only talk to us as we approach our deaths, but if Sayer is to be believed our parallel selves are never in the same condition.

The problem appeared to me as a symbol for all the inequality this nowhere represented, the simple unfairness that its existence embodied. They looked down their noses at us, but we suffer the burdens of having to live in a world that is not utopia, and furthermore of dying in a world that is not utopia.

Sayer contemplated, sipping his tea from my bone china. 'I do not know. I have never even been able to work out why they contact people in your condition.'

'I'm dying, Sayer, there's no need for euphemisms.'

'Yes, quite,' he answered, looking at my red carpet. 'Some of the others had their own theories, would you like to know? I mean, it's speculative, I've never heard of a letter from nowhere that goes into it.'

'Yes, I'd like to know.'

'I'm not even sure how much they know about us, about the people they are corresponding with. Other than that they are talking to alternative versions of themselves, who come from a world a little like the one of their past.'

'Please, Sayer, tell me what the others thought.'

'One women, who was quite religious, a Muslim actually, thought that they were Djinn—the third sapient creations of God who exist in something like a parallel reality and have free-will. That they were mischievous, but not unkind, and that they were trying to offer pleasant stories to the dying, but they were just pretending to be our doubles, as a part of the stories. And the society they described was probably an idealised version of Djinn society. I liked that explanation.'

'I guess it makes as much sense as the letters from nowhere themselves.'

'Well, another guy, this old bloke who used to drive trucks, he took the letters more at face-value and he thought that maybe we were the dream lives of these denizens of nowhere, in some kind of shared unconscious. And that these dream selves are dying because the part of our consciousness that is separated from our true selves is waking up.'

'I'm not sure that makes sense.'

Sayer shrugged and smiled his wonky smile. 'There was one child, I met her only a few times on an oncology ward. Her parents approached me after finding my website. She said something that disturbed me. That these letter writers were stealing our lives. That they made their wonderful world out of the life we don't get to live. They were sort of vampires to her, a world of vampires.'

'I feel a lot like that. When I read the letters, that's often how I feel.'

Sayer shrugged. 'I'm sorry Carol.'

'It must be hard for you to do this? To go around talking to the dying all of the time? No?'

'I don't mind. I wouldn't have thought of doing it without the letters. If my nephew… well.'

A silence encroached on our conversation and threatened to swallow it up.

'Did he get the letters?' I asked.

Sayer nodded, his smile this time was forced, closed-mouthed. 'He was wonderful. I didn't believe him, my brother still doesn't. We don't talk about all this, what I do. But I need to know, right? And I wonder, maybe one day I will get a letter too.'

One week Sayer couldn't visit. He had to man his store. Those two weeks went slowly, not helped by some dull letters from nowhere. My utopian self could become as stuck on tangents as Sayer, and all she wanted to write about for that fortnight was her love of Parisian arcades and coffee culture.

I suspected that she lacked a clear motive for communicating and saw it more as a pen pal set-up than a means to communicate about their society. Even Bernard had abandoned me. He had been vomiting on the carpets, the smell of strong, lemony antibacterial cleaner perforated my living room. Rather than always taking Bernard back to mine, some days Samantha kept him at her and Joseph's house, which was closer to the poor old thing's vet.

As a consequence, that one Sunday I had no visitor at all and felt a terrifying isolation, almost a vertigo.

When I did next see Sayer, it was as though he had saved up two visits worth of information to express at once. He was keener to talk about utopias than the letters. 'Their decadence reminds me a bit of... yes, E. M. Forster's *The Machine Stops*, or... or...' he clicked his fingers in annoyance, summoning the right book. 'Oh, Michael Moorcock! *Dancers at the End of Time*. But it's different, those fictional societies had no material needs and spent their time on cultural pursuits, but they weren't creative. They plagiarised and commented, like me, they were just critics and literary theorists. They were moved only by nostalgia. And in our nowhere, there's plenty of nostalgia, but all mixed up with originality. With new movements in music, paintings, writing, even new scents and fashions.

'What is it your Carol is always saying? History didn't end, right, it began. They don't see our history as history proper. They study it as kind of an anomaly, like we study pre-history. Before language, before paradise. And they believe, perhaps justifiably, that we aren't as fully human as them.'

'I hate that about them,' I interrupted.

'But they can't help it. They relate to the world and to each other on such a different plateau.'

'I hate them.' I was still angry about my long loneliness. But Sayer's enthusiasm robbed my voice of its conviction.

He changed the subject. 'You see, a utopia doesn't just mean some ideal society. It's more than that, its about better institutions.' I had heard this tangent before.

I do not believe in silver linings. Sure, a young man crippled before a war might be spared conscription, but then both conscription and disability are evils and these turns of fate do not change that essential suffering.

But Sayer, he believed in silver linings. And many of our arguments centred on this disagreement.

'Not everything is resolved for them,' he would say. 'They might have got society down, but they still die and age. They still have unrequited love. The very ingenuity of their solutions to human yearnings such as envy and despair show that these remain obstacles in their lives. Perhaps this nowhere is a utopia, but it seems to me that utopia only addresses the practical problems in a human life.

'And how depressing is it that we are still so burdened by these practical problems that for many, most, the urgent problems—the incontrovertible fact of our deaths, the enjoyment of beauty, how we form and maintain real bonds—are reduced to idle luxuries for the few to work out during their lives? They, your other Carol, are blessed, because they get to suffer in a more human way than we do.'

I rejected his argument. 'I resent what you call their decadence, but isn't it really more of a childishness than decadence? And isn't that childishness, that awe for the big problems of being human, isn't that a very hollow consolation for suffering and illness and death?'

Our arguments would always end up unresolved. But in that ellipsis, I was somehow always revived, for a time.

Five months after meeting Sayer, a fortnight after I received my last letter from the other Carol, he and I married in a quiet ceremony in my town's council building. Then, I moved to his home in London. He had a bedroom with high ceilings and bay windows, and there he had a writing desk set up for me. The room was fitted with state of the art medical equipment beeping and buzzing around the bed.

Bernard stayed with beautiful Samantha, whom I felt would benefit from his tail wagging canine company more than I. My hope is that the poor mutt outlives me.

And it is here, in Sayer's room, that I wrote this short account. Nowadays, I keep thinking of those tableaus in the shop window, the idealised life they suggest, and how nobody in my world seems to really live a life suited to such a setting.

It's a thought that makes me resent the other Carol a little less.

Writing Prompts from Nowhere

…work is illegal. People work, but only with the detached irony of a child's game. The punishment for work is summary execution without due process, but it is never enforced because, as Yoko Tawada understands:

Nothing is more frightening than a law that has never been enforced.

…people are encouraged to meditate and pray daily, for long periods, and especially to guard against productivity. Any attempt to justify such activities—or explain what they accomplish—is treated like someone audibly farting in a confined space.

…there is an official state religion and the others are relentlessly persecuted. This is chosen at random each year, with every faith written on a piece of paper, folded and selected out of the prime minister's favourite hat. The chosen paper is burned, before even the prime minister is permitted to see it. To qualify for entry into the hat, a child must freely profess belief in the faith.

….there is no class system, and every member is regarded a priest, deserving the highest social status.

…a great metropolis is built in the geographical centre. It is five times the size of the second largest city, opulently designed with gold inlay and baroque, neoclassical and perpendicular architecture, juxtaposed without uniformity. The place is unpopulated, but everyone regards its hypothetical residents as the worst sort, and the city as a Sodom or Tower of Babel, a place of sin, hubris, decadence and moral catastrophe. It is held up as everything wrong and the faithful wonder why God does not smite it, immolating every man, woman and child within. People ask, 'does even one good person reside there?' to which they would be answered, truthfully, 'no.'

…launderettes, hair salons and post office queues are the primary spheres of adult socialisation. Despite technology rendering such places (and their attendant domain specific activities) obsolete, all but the most ardent quietists and dogmatic introverts regularly attend them.

…all cities are garden cities. Botany is a blessed profession and the imbibing of botany-derived alcoholic drinks is accompanied by prayers of gratitude for the continuity of the science.

…everyone is burdened with the debt of every human being who has ever, and will ever, exist. This debt is owed to the youngest member of society and, were this person to collect on what is rightly theirs, society would collapse. Fortunately, it has yet to happen.

…pessimism (especially anti-natalism and Malthusianism) is taboo and enforced against by a violent and secret police. However, this law enforcement organisation is pre-theoretical, employing nobody and without an allocated budget. And despite prohibitions against philosophical despair, pathos and wistfulness, all instances of delicate sadness are venerated, with statues personifying the emotions as well as highly attended temples and roadside shrines to honour them. Sufferers of such conditions are especially revered, albeit from an acceptable distance for reasons obscurely related to public health.

...modesty is loathed as an intolerable conceit and vanity. Anybody—of any gender—found in public without a coherent and individual style and a cultivated, unique theory of aesthetics reflected in each aspect of their lives, is laughed at for the absurd self-regard of imagining their unadorned selves sufficient. They are derided as embarrassing examples of human-peacocks.

...the teaching and learning of hermeneutics and jurisprudence is heavily state subsidised. Conferences, seminars, journals and lectures operate perpetually even in the smallest, most remote hamlets. However, the focus of these disciplines is only to make sacred text and the law harder to interpret and understand.

...academics and intellectuals are periodically purged in an obscene and bloodthirsty festival of carnage. This is done to keep philosophers, historians, linguists, anthropologists, theologians and so on courageous and serious in their work. It is also used to abate humanity's depravity. The exact date of the purge is permanently suspended, with the official reason being that weather conditions do not allow the proper enjoyment of planned activities. Parents are encouraged to both praise and mourn their children when they choose academic vocations.

...there is a great proliferation of law and lawyers. Studying the law is heavily encouraged, but cataloguing or implementing laws is regarded as in the poorest taste.

...there are no permanent restaurants, but a great number of theatrical pop-up eateries. Participation is held up as a spiritual and martial exercise of discipline and self-cultivation, an honouring of the prehistorical days before utopia. Pop-up restaurants happen anywhere, including private residences. And they happen at any time. Many have been woken at 3am to find large numbers using their homes to honour the ancestors with three courses of fusion cuisine, each course modelled on a 20th-century *avant-garde* art movement

...the defence budget is fully expended on researching the coming expansion, in which society will take up arms against neighbouring countries, forming northern, eastern, western and southern fronts, and enforcing the ideals of utopia on the world. This is so expensive and employs so many people that the production of armaments and building the necessary infrastructure for war is never possible.

...archery and quarterstaff training on the local green is mandatory. Quarterstaff duals are encouraged in matters of passion, during which everybody settles conflicts of lust, friendship and romance. Participants are plied with drink, feasts, dancing and more duals, celebrated for weeks and kept awake as long as possible with merriment, usually with the consequence that after all festivities any memory of the altercation is forgotten and the exhausted triumphant freely staggers arm-in-arm with his adversary for a period of austere and welcome recuperation.

...people outdo one another with abstract expressionist portraits, concrete poetry and improv theatre. One's standing and aesthetic expression is as whimsical and interrelated as wealth and status were in former societies.

...nothing is more hated than pseudo-rebellion. Artists who make facile, vague, abstract, boring, passé, trite, nice, cute, forced, contrived, platitudinal or empty critiques of society will be re-educated until their art becomes unsettling, challenging and baffling.

…nothing is regarded as more pitiable than someone who exploits themselves. Sobs of empathy and horror accompany such fools wherever they go about their lives.

…all people are encouraged to write utopias throughout their lives. Entire relationships are predicated on the exchange of utopian visions and more utopias are produced in a single hour than any person could read in a hundred lifetimes. Utopias are given as holiday gifts and to celebrate life events, in gratitude and out of spite, for no reason and any.

I have said before on my blog—and elsewhere too—that premises are cheap; they are merely the framework for your story, the scaffolding that allow us as writers to explore our more important and difficult thematic concerns. I stand by this. Nonetheless, they can get us going and it can be helpful to find them from outside of our own minds, to push us in usual directions and overcome tired ways of thinking.

Utopia is a neglected but justly proud genre, and there are many potentially great bases on which to write one. Here are ten examples, which you can draw from, blend, or perversely ignore in favour of something you conceived or found elsewhere.

1. Blake's Dialectical Utopia
   'It indeed appear'd to Reason as if Desire was cast out; but the Devil's account is, that the Messiah fell, and formed a Heaven of what he stole from the Abyss.' — William Blake

2. A Utopia of Sickness

The joys of the disease were so many that ultimately, the quarantine was erected as much—if not more—to keep people outside of the city than to keep them inside of it.

3. A Society of Friends

Friendship meant that our affection was not based on any—even implied—exchange. Because we recovered the commons, and nobody suffered from any unmet needs, our society was one of universal friendship.

4. A Dying Paradise

The earth was imminently condemned, but in the face of that apocalypse, peace and happiness were established. At its very end, humanity spontaneously became human.

5. Dual Power

Once most of society became surplus to the economy's requirements, we built a paradise and allowed the old society to simply wither away by itself. New institutions existed parallel to the old, which became less and less relevant until they were forgotten altogether.

6. Marx's Communist Utopia

'In communist society, where nobody has one exclusive sphere of activity but each can become accomplished in any branch he wishes, society regulates the general production and thus makes it possible for me to do one thing today and another tomorrow, to hunt in the morning, fish in the afternoon, rear cattle in the evening, criticise after dinner, just as I have a mind, without ever becoming hunter, fisherman, shepherd or critic.'— Karl Marx

7. Utopian Play

What was unique about their performance? What gave it this strange power, that meant that everywhere this troupe appeared utopia soon arrived too? Nobody knew, but all welcomed the players as they might an army liberating them from occupation.

8. Nowhere in Space

On our star chart the strange purple planet—the inhabitable world on the outer fringes of known space—was marked simply 'Nowhere.' This was our destination, we were going nowhere, fast.

9. Le Guin's Yin Utopia

'What would a yin utopia be? It would be dark, wet, obscure, weak, yielding, passive, participatory, circular, cyclical, peaceful, nurturant, retreating, contracting and cold.' — Ursula K. Le Guin

10. The Final Protest

It began as a celebratory protest, but soon it took on its own forms of distribution, its own institutions of justice and cooperative work, and as more and more people joined with this permanent festival, it became the same as society itself.

Appendices

Pre-Utopia

c. 1940 BC: [Anonymous] 'The Tale of the Shipwrecked Sailor' (poem) (Egypt)

c. 340–380 BC: Plato, *The Republic* (Greece)
— Although not a utopia in the sense of More's book (as it lacks any fictional component and is not realised as a living world), Plato's *Republic* is unquestionably the most influential book on the genre, and plenty of its features (especially its static conception, golden lie, communism and orderliness) remained hallmarks of the genre long after More, arguably only being critiqued and developed in the nineteenth century.

c. 300 BC: Zeno of Citium, *The Republic* (Greece)
— A Stoic ideal commonwealth, along the lines of Plato's *Republic*. Not extant.

c. 300 BC: Euhemerus, *Sacred History* (Greece)
— This text describes a rational island paradise named Panchaea. Not extant.

c. 165–50 BC: Iambulus, *Islands of the Sun* (Greece)
— Allegedly another Stoic ideal commonwealth, also along the lines of Plato's Republic. Not extant.

98: Tacitus, *Germanica* (Italy)

c. 100: Plutarch, *Life of Lycurgus* (Greece)

c. 400: Augustine of Hippo, *The City of God* (Algeria)
— More a philosophical or theological text than a utopia, it nonetheless features utopian conceptions.

421: Tao Yuanming, 'Peach Blossom Springs' (poem) (China)
— Fictional depiction of an ideal state, debatably anticipating More. It's quite thin on details, but does feature strong utopian ideas about the abolition of tax and regulated agriculture. It also has elements of a Cockaygne type fantasy.

c. 874–950: Al-Farabi, *The Virtuous City* (Al-Madina al-Fadila) (Iraq)

The Renaissance 1300–1700

c. 1300. [Anonymous] 'The Land of Cokaygne' (Ireland) (poem)
— Part of a genre depicting paradisal lands of plenty, anticipating post-scarcity SF and arguably surpassed by the more realised visions of More et al.

1404: Christine de Pizan, *The Book of the City of Ladies* (Italy)
— An allegory in which the titular city is the book itself, which is a home for noteworthy women so as to exemplify women's accomplishments throughout history. Although not utopian in More's sense, it anticipates his work with its idea of a model city demonstrating virtue.

Post-Utopia

1516: Thomas More, *Utopia* (England)
- — Containing elements of the later utopia, dystopia & anti-utopia fiction, the clearest progenitor of the genre and still one of the greatest works of its kind.

The Reformation (1517–1648)

1521: Johann Eberlin von Günzburg, *Wolfaria* (Germany)

1532: Niccolò Machiavelli, *The Prince* (Italy)
- — Satire on misgovernment, commonly misinterpreted as a blueprint for modernist tyranny.

1549: Étienne de La Boétie, *The Discourse on Voluntary Servitude, or the Against-One* (France)
- — An essay by Montaigne's closest friend (somewhat touched on in the *Essays*), it anticipates anarchist theory.

1553: Francesco Patrizi, *La Città felice* (Croatia)

1559: Joannes Ferrarius Montanus, *A Work touching the Good Ordering of a Common Weal* (Germany)

c. 1580: Michel de Montaigne, *Essays* (in particular, 'Of Cannibals') (France)

1589: Giovanni Botero, *The Reason of State* (Italy)
- — Botero critiques the misinterpreted reading of *The Prince*, arguing against Machiavelli's satire of amoral governance. More importantly, it is one of many anti-Aristotelian texts, which was a motif of the Renaissance that would carry right through to the Enlightenment. Campanella, Andreae, Bacon and Plattes can all be seen in this anti-Aristotelian (and implicitly pro-Platonic) tradition, which

simplifies the legacy of Plato and Aristotle. This also, importantly, connects to both the Reformation and Counter-Reformation.

1600s: Thomas Traherne, *Centuries of Meditations* (England)

1602: Tommaso Campanella, *The City of the Sun* (Italy)
— Heretical catholic utopia, influenced by neoplatonism (possibly Hermeticism). Strongly anticipates or influenced its protestant counterpart, *Christianopolis*.

1615: Lodovico Zuccolo, *Il Belluzzi o vero della citta felice* (Italy)

1616: Jean de Moncy, *Histoire du grand et admirable royaume d'Antangil* (France)

1619: Johannes Valentinus Andreae, *Christianopolis* (Germany)
— One of the best early utopias, by one of the supposed founders of the secret occult society of Rosicrucianism. There is significant textual evidence that this book influenced Bacon's *New Atlantis*. It is the most imaginative and richly conceived work since More and arguably until Swift.

1625: Lodovico Zuccolo, *La Repubblica d'Evandria* (Italy)

1627: Francis Bacon *New Atlantis* (England)
— Arguably the first technological utopia, and one of the most influential utopias of its time.

c. 1620 (p. 1638): Francis Godwin, *The Man in the Moone* (England)

1641: Gabriel Plattes (not Samuel Hartlib), *The Description of the Famous Kingdom of Macaria* (England)

The English Civil War (1642–51)

1648: Samuel Gott. *Nova Solyma, sive Institutio Christiani* (England)

The Trial & Execution of Charles I (1649)

1651: Thomas Hobbes, *Leviathan* (England)
— Philosophical work outlining social contract theory and ideal governance.

1652: Gerrard Winstanley, *The Law of Freedom in a Platform* (England)
— Debatably the first modern practical utopia.

c. 1653–94: François Rabelais, *Gargantua and Pantagruel* (France)

1656: James Harrington, *The Commonwealth of Oceana* (England)
— Written on the night of Charles I's execution, dedicated to Oliver Cromwell, this was the most influential utopia of its time (perhaps any time) and provided ideas that would shape the division of powers in the US and provide a reference point for utopias all the way to David Hume's *Idea of a Perfect Commonwealth* nearly a century later and Cabet's utopia nearly two centuries later—and arguably, through Cabet, it helped to shape socialist ideas too.

1657: Cyrano de Bergerac, *Comical History of the States and Empires of the Moon* (France)

1660: John Sadler, *Olbia: The New Island Lately Discovered* (England)

1660: R. H. Esquire (pseudonym), *New Atlantis: Continued by R. H. Esquire* (England)

1666: Margaret Cavendish, *The Blazing World* (England)
   — First utopia written by a woman.

1668: Henry Neville, *The Isle of the Pines* (England)

1676: Gabriel de Foigny, *The Southern Land Known* (France)

1675: Denis Vairasse, *The history of the Sevarites or Sevarambi* (France)

1676: Joseph Glanvill Antifanatickal, *Religion & Free Philosophy: Continuation of the New Atlantis* (England)

1682: [Anonymous] *Description of the Sinapia, peninsula in the Southern Land* (Spain)

1699: Francois de Salignac de la Mothe Fenelon, *The Adventures of Telemachus* (France)

1709: [Anonymous] *The Island of Content: or, A New Paradise Discovered* (England)

The Enlightenment (1715–89)

1719: Daniel Defoe, *Robinson Crusoe* (England)

1720: [Anonymous] *A Description of New Athens in Terra Australis Incognita* (England)

1726: Jonathan Swift, *Gulliver's Travels* (England/Ireland)
   — Encompasses utopian and anti-utopian speculation.

1738: Simon Berington, *The memoirs of Signor Gaudentio di Lucca* (England)

1751: Robert Paltock, *The Life and Adventures of Peter Wilkins* (England)

1752: David Hume, *Idea of a Perfect Commonwealth* (Scotland)

1753: William Smith, *A General Idea of the College of Mirania* (America)

1754: Jean-Jacques Rousseau, *Discourse on the Origin and Basis of Inequality Among Men* (France)
— Rousseau is a key influence on the Enlightenment, The French Revolution, and the formation of the left; he is also, therefore, a key figure in the development of utopian fiction.

1759: Samuel Johnson, *Rasselas* (England)

1759: Voltaire, *Candide* (France)
— Only the El Dorado section of *Candide*; although generally not written in a utopian vain, this book is nonetheless full of utopian as well as anti-utopian ideas.

1752: Voltaire, *Micromégas*

1762: Jean-Jacques Rousseau, *The Social Contract*

1762: Sarah Scott, *Millenium Hall*

1764: James Burgh, *An Account of the Cessares*

1771: Louis-Sébastien Mercier, *Memoirs of the Year Two Thousand Five Hundred*

1772: Denis Diderot, *Supplément au voyage de Bougainville*

The American Revolutionary War (1775–83)
The French Revolution (1789–99)

1782: Thomas Spence, *A Supplement to the History of Robinson Crusoe* (England)

c. 1789: William Blake, *Tiriel* (England)

c. 1789: William Blake, *The Book of Thel*

1793: William Blake, *America a Prophecy*

1793: William Blake, *Visions of the Daughters of Albion*

1793: William Godwin, *Enquiry Concerning Political Justice* (England)

1794: William Blake, *The Book of Urizen*

1794: William Blake, *Europe a Prophecy*

1794: Thomas Spence, *A Marine Republic, or A Description of Spensonia*

1795: William Blake, *The Book of Ahania*

1795: William Blake, *The Book of Los*

1795: William Blake, *The Song of Los*

1795: William Hodgson, *The Commonwealth of Reason* (England)

1795: Thomas Northmore, *Memoirs of Planetes* (England)

1798: Thomas Robert Malthus, *An Essay on the Principle of Population* (England)
  — Explicitly anti-utopian and reactionary (written, in part, as a rebuttal to William Godwin), many utopian writers (especially when not influenced by Marx), treated the 'problem' of overpopulation seriously. One of the most explicitly anti-Malthusian texts is not a utopia, but Charles Dickens's 1843 novella, *A Christmas Carol*.

1798: Thomas Spence, *The Constitution of a Perfect Commonwealth*

1801: Thomas Spence, *The Constitution of Spensonia: A Country in Fairyland Situated Between Utopia and Oceana*

1802: [Anonymous] *Bruce's Voyage to Naples* (England)

1803: Henri de Saint-Simon, *Lettres d'un habitant de Genève à ses contemporains* (France)
  — Outlining his utopian socialism. Saint-Simon was one of three authors Engels references in *Socialism: Utopian and Scientific*.

c. 1804: William Blake, *Vala, or The Four Zoas*

1804–10: William Blake, *Milton a Poem*

1804–20: William Blake, *Jerusalem The Emanation of the Giant Albion*

1805: Thomas Spence, *The Receipt to Make a Millenium or Happy World*

The Napoleonic Wars (1803–15)

1808: Charles Fourier, *Theory of the Four Movements* (France)
— Outlining his utopian socialism. Fourier was one of three authors Engels references in *Socialism: Utopian and Scientific*.

1811: James Henry Lawrence, *The Empire of the Nairs* (?)

1813 Robert Owen, *A New View of Society* (Wales)
— Outlining his utopian socialism. Owen was one of three authors Engels references in Socialism: Utopian and Scientific.

The Peterloo Massacre (1819)

1819: Percy Bysshe Shelley, *The Masque of Anarchy* (poem) (England)

1820: Percy Bysshe Shelley, *Prometheus Unbound*

1836:Mary Griffith, *Three Hundred Years Hence* (America)

1838: [Various] *The People's Charter* (England)
— The founding document of Chartism, a working-class political reformist movement that flourished between 1838–57.

1840: Nathaniel Hawthorne, *The Blithedale Romance* (America)
— A satire of Hawthorne's experiences of living in a utopian commune, this book is nonetheless ambivalent and sometimes generous to the experiment.

1840: Étienne Cabet, *Travels in Icaria* (France)
— Cabet's Christian communalism and communism was both influenced by, and influenced, Marx. Although his utopia is very simplistic, and utterly implausible in its absolutist interpretation of egalitarianism.

1840: Pierre-Joseph Proudhon, *What is Property?* (France)
— Important work in the development of anarchism; discounting La Boétie, it is perhaps the founding text of modern anarchism—although it's central claim, that property is theft, would be mocked as self-refuting by otherwise opposing philosophers Marx and Stirner.

c. 1841–5: John Goodwyn Barmby, *The Book of Platonopolis* (England)
— Chartist utopia with strong neoplatonist ideas, not extant and likely somewhat derivative of Étienne Cabet's *Travels in Icaria.*

1844: Max Stirner, *The Ego and Its Own* (Germany)
— Important work in the development of individualistic anarchism, Stirner's Hegelian Egoism drew criticisms from Marx and would influence the ideas of Ayn Rand.

1848: Fredrika Bremer, *Sibling Life or Brothers and Sisters* (Sweden)

1848: Karl Marx, *The Communist Manifesto* (Germany)
— Marxism opposes previous utopianism for two, interrelated reasons: the inevitable failure to perceive a historical class-based dialectic that could serve as the basis for revolution and bring about the new society, for which utopians are not blamed, and the conception of an ideal society as static along the model supplied by Plato and More. Nonetheless, Marxism is more compatible with later conceptions of utopianism as mutable and revolutionary.

The American Civil War (1861–65)

1858: Joseph Déjacque, *L'Humanisphère, Utopie anarchique* (France)
— Déjacque, an anarcho-communist, coined the term libertarian. This book is perhaps the first truly anarchist utopia.

1867: Henrik Ibsen, *Peer Gynt* (Norway)
— This play features details from a Norwegian fairytale that has Cockaygne-typical features.

Unification of Germany
Paris Commune (1871)

1871: Edward Bulwer-Lytton, *The Coming Race* (England)
— With its depictions of genocide and other horrors, and its whimsical author, it is questionable how this book and its ideas were meant to be interpreted, but it seems unlikely that it was intended as straightforwardly utopian. As an MP, his politics moved from Whig (1831–1841) to Tory (1851–1866).

1872: Samuel Butler, *Erewhon* (England)
— Arguably an anti-utopia, it nonetheless features utopian ideas.

1873: Mikhail Bakunin, *Statism and Anarchy* (Russia)
— After Proudhon, another seminal work in the development of anarchism.

1873: Louisa May Alcott, *Transcendental Wild Oats* (short story) (America)

1875: Karl Marx, *Critique of the Gotha Programme*

1879: Henry George, *Progress and Poverty* (America)
— Georgism (the ideas of Henry George) states that all value derived from land (or any natural resource with a limited supply) should belong to everyone in society as a justification for a single tax. This is both a moral and an economic argument, with roots in Lockeian presuppositions.

1880: Friedrich Engels, *Socialism: Utopian and Scientific* (England)
— Distinguishes between Marxism (scientific socialism) and utopian socialism (i.e. the socialism of Henri de Saint-Simon, Charles Fourier and Robert Owen, who Engels argues did not derive their ideas from material and historical conditions). Karl Popper would misunderstand the distinction in an attempt to dub socialism a pseudoscience by submitting it to his different (and controversial) conception of the scientific method.

1880: Percy Greg, *Across the Zodiac* (England)
— Anti-communist response to Bellamy, with dystopian and utopian elements.

1880–1 (serialised): Mary Bradley Lane, *Mizora* (America)
- — Perhaps the first of the true feminist utopias, *Mizora* anticipates elements of Dixie, Corbett, Rokeya and Gilman's fictions.

1883 John 'Ismar Thiusen' Macnie, *The Diothas; or, A Far Look Ahead* (Scotland)
- — Huge influence on the better known *Looking Backward* by Edward Bellamy, and arguably the most influential of all the forgotten utopias.

1887: W. H. Hudson, *A Crystal Age* (Argentina)
- — One of the most ambiguous 'utopias' of the nineteenth century, it was perhaps more meant as a speculative fable about gender and familial organisation.

1887: Lillie Blake, 'A Divided Republic' (short story) (America)

1887: Anna Bowman Dodd, *The Republic of the Future* (America)
- — Although technically a dystopia, its descriptions of socialist America are not all that off-putting.

1888: Edward Bellamy, *Looking Backward: 2000–1887* (America)
- — Edward Bellamy is the most influential utopian of the 19th Century and helped inspire many future utopian texts, positively (see Corbett, Donnelly, Chavannes, Chauncey Thomas, Hertzka, Wells, Gilman) and, perhaps more importantly, negatively (see Morris).

1889: Elizabeth Burgoyne Corbett, *New Amazonia: A Foretaste of the Future* (England)
- — Many features of the future matriarchy in this story (which is authoritarian, Malthusian and

114

puritanical) are presented ambivalently. One of the early feminist utopias.

1890: Theodor Hertzka, *Freeland* (Hungary)

1890: Lady Florence, *Dixie Gloriana, or the Revolution of 1900* (Scotland)
— Early feminist utopia.

1890: Ignatius Donnelly, *Cæsar's Column: a Story of the Twentieth Century* (America)
— More an anti-capitalist satire, Donnelly was one of the strangest of left-leaning conspiracists, but the book is perhaps worth reading for its operatic melodrama and shocking conclusion.

1890: William Morris, *News from Nowhere* (England)
— Putting aside Cabet's complex example, Morris was the first acknowledged Marxist to write a true utopia in the tradition of More. Alongside More, Andreae, Huxley, Le Guin, Piercy and Shawl, Morris is one of the greatest utopian authors in terms of literary and visionary merit.

1891: Chauncey Thomas, *The Crystal Button* (America)

1891: Conrad Wilbrandt, *Mr. East's Experiences in Mr. Bellamy's World: Records of the Years 2001 and 2002* (Germany)

1892: Albert Chavannes, *The Future Commonwealth* (Switzerland/America)

1892–3 (serialised): William Dean Howells, *A Traveller from Altruria* (America)

1893: Eugene Richter, *Pictures of the Socialistic Future*

1893: Alice Ilgenfritz Jones & Ella Merchant, *Unveiling a Parallel* (America)

1894: Walter Browne, *2894, or The Fossil Man (A Midwinter Night's Dream)* (America)

1895: Albert Chavannes, *In Brighter Climes*

1897: Edward Bellamy, *Equality* (America)

1889: Edward Carpenter, 'Civilisation: Its Cause and Cure' (poem)(England)

1898: Kārlis 'Ballod-Atlanticus' Balodis, *The Future State* (Latvia)

1898: H. G. Wells, *The Sleeper Awakes* (England)

1899: Anna Adolph, *Arqtiq* (America)

1900: [Anonymous] *My Afterdream. A Sequel to the Late Mr. Bellamy's Looking Backward* (England)

1900: Alconoan O. Grigsby & Mary P. Lowe, *NEQUA or The Problem of the Ages* (America)

1901: H. G. Wells, *The First Men in the Moon*

1904: G. K. Chesterton, *The Napoleon of Notting Hill* (England)

1905: Edward Carpenter, 'Towards Democracy' (poem)

1905: Anatole France The White Stone (France)

1905: Gabriel Tarde Underground Man (France)

1905: Rokeya Sakhawat 'Begum Rokeya' Hussain 'Sultana's Dream' (short story) (Bangladesh)

1905: H. G. Wells, *A Modern Utopia*

1906: H. G. Wells, *In the Days of the Comet*

1907: Ernest Bramah, *What Might Have Been: The Story of a Social War*

1907: Robert Blatchford, *The Sorcery Shop* (England)

1907: Jack London, *The Iron Heel* (America)

1908: Alexander Bogdanov, *Red Star* (Russia)

1911: Charlotte Perkins Gilman, *Moving the Mountain* (America)

1911: H. G. Wells, *The New Machiavelli*

1913: Charlotte Perkins Gilman, 'Bee Wise' (short story)

1914: H. G. Wells, *The World Set Free*

World War I (1914–18)

During this period dystopias began to eclipse utopias in popularity. The period leading up to, between and after the world wars saw the publication of the seminal texts of this (debatably) new genre: *The Iron Heel* (1908) by Jack London, *The Machine Stops* (1909) by E. M. Forster, *We* (1921) by Yevgeny Zamyatin, *Brave New World* (1932) by Aldous Huxley, *It Can't Happen Here* (1935) by Sinclair Lewis, *Swastika Night* (1937) by Katharine Burdekin and (arguably the most derivative but most influential), *Nineteen Eighty-Four* (1949) by George Orwell. These books were written as criticisms of fascism/oligarchy London, Huxley, Lewis, Burdekin) or totalitarian socialism (Zamyatin and Orwell). However, utopias continued to be written, and sometimes by the same authors (London's *The Iron Heel* even contains the rudiments of a post-oligarchic utopia and Huxley, Lewis and Burdekin all wrote noteworthy utopian novels). Furthermore, attributing the decline of the utopia to this period and the rise of authoritarian /totalitarian politics is ahistorical (utopias have thrived in times of violence and ideological tumult, through revolutions and religious wars).

117

1915: Charlotte Perkins Gilman, *Herland*

1916: Charlotte Perkins Gilman, *With Her in Our Land*

1916: Lillian B. Jones Horace, *Five Generations Hence* (America)
— First known utopia written by a black American woman.

The Russian Revolution (1917)

1918: Oliver Onions, *The New Moon: A Romance of Reconstruction* (England)

1922: Alexander Moszkowski, *The Islands of Wisdom* (Germany)

1922: H. G. Wells, *Men Like Gods*

1924: Upton Sinclair, *The Millennium: A Comedy of the Year 2000* (America)

1924: Rose Macaulay, *Rose Island*

1927: J.B.S. Haldane, *The Last Judgement* (England)

1928: Haywire Mac, 'The Big Rock Candy Mountain' (America) (song)
— One version of an American folk song, which is itself derivative of the Cockaygne story.

1933: James Hilton, *Lost Horizon* (England)

1935 (published 1989): Katherine Burdekin, *The End of This Day's Business* (England)

1935: Herbert Read, *The Green Child* (England)

1935: H. G. Wells, *The Shape of Things to Come*

1936: Karel Čapek, *War with the Newts* (Czechia)
— More satire than utopia, it nonetheless features utopian themes.

World War II (1939–45)

1938 (p. 2003) Robert A. Heinlein, *For Us, The Living: A Comedy of Customs* (America)

1942: Lord Samuel, *An Unknown Lan*d (England)

1942: Austin Tappan Wright, *Islandia* (America)

1943: Hermann Hesse, *The Glass Bead Game* (Germany)

1943: Aleister Crowley 'The City of God: A Rhapsody' (poem) (England)

1945: H. G. Wells, *Mind at the End of Its Tether*

UK National Insurance Act (1946)

1948: B. F. Skinner, *Walden Two* (America)

1949: T. H. Marshall, *Citizenship and Social Class* (England)
— Provides the theoretical underpinnings for the social liberal welfare state.

1954: Arthur C. Clarke, *Childhood's End* (England)

1954–9 (3 volumes): Ernst Bloch, *The Principle of Hope*
— A seminal Marxist account of utopia, which broadens the definition in such a way as to give the concept new depth and meaning artistically and politically.

1962: Aldous Huxley, *Island* (England)

1966: Ursula K. Le Guin, *Planet of Exile* (America)
— Le Guin can be said to usher in the 1970s utopian revival, this period would introduce a less static conception of utopias as anticipated by Marxist historian A. L. Morton (what would be dubbed process utopias) as well as utopias focussing largely on feminism, ecology and political ambiguity

(perhaps postmodern in various senses). It survives until the 80s and what some regard as a new economic-political consensus)

1967: Ursula K. Le Guin, *City of Illusions*

1967: Poul Anderson, 'Eutopia' (short story) (America)

The Invention of ARPANET (1969)

1969: Ursula K. Le Guin, *The Left Hand of Darkness*

1970: Joanna Russ, *The Female Man* (America)

1974: J.G. Ballard, *Concrete Island* (England)

1974: Suzy McKee Charnas, *Walk to the End of the World* (America)

1974:Ursula K. Le Guin, *The Dispossessed*

1975: J.G. Ballard, *High-Rise*
— While this and *Concrete Island* better fit the anti-utopian sub-genre, Ballard retains a modernist utopianism that belies some of his dark subject matter and social critique.

1975: Julio Cortázar, *Fantomas versus the Multinational Vampire: An Attainable Utopia* (Argentina)
— Less a utopia than a defence of the idea of utopia, this comic book is clever and highly of its time.

1975: Ernest Callenbach, *Ecotopia* (America)

1976: Samuel R. Delany, *Triton* (America)
— Influenced by Le Guin and the French philosopher Michel Foucault, this is arguably the most postmodern and ambiguous of the 70s utopias.

1976: Marge Piercy, *Woman on the Edge of Time* (America)
— The greatest of the 70s utopias.

1978: Suzy McKee Charnas, *Motherlines*

1979: Sally Miller Gearhart, *The Wanderground* (America)

Thatcher/Reagan Era or TINA (1979–90)
Fall of the Berlin Wall (1989)

The Utopia is dead, long live Utopia! The commencement of the '80s is often seen as the culmination of the decline of the genre in its death, sometimes attributed to Reaganism/Thatcherism, the Fall of the Berlin Wall, and cemented by Clintonism/Blairism Third Way politics. Nonetheless, many utopias can still be found, and given the so-called Literary Inundation (John Sutherland's idea that the global population explosion has produced greater and greater quantities of text) it would be surprising had any genre truly died. Rather, the utopia has become more disconnected, with authors less in conversation with one another, less consciously aware of belonging to a literary tradition. There is also a greater concern with post-scarcity fantasies (see Banks, Robinson, Clarke). Insofar as post-scarcity SF corresponds to the Cockaygne stories, this can be seen as the genre returning to its pre-Utopia origins in folk stories.

1979: Doris Lessing, *Shikasta* (England/Zimbabwe)

1980: Doris Lessing, *The Marriages Between Zones 3, 4 and 5*

1980: Doris Lessing, *The Sirian Experiments*

1980: L. Neil Smith, *The Probability Broach* (America)
— Rare example of a right-wing libertarian utopia.

121

1981: Ernest Callenbach, *Ecotopia Emerging*

1982: Doris Lessing, *The Making of the Representative for Planet 8*

1982: James P. Hogan, *Voyage from Yesteryear* (England)

1983: Doris Lessing, *The Sentimental Agents in the Volyen*

1985: Ursula K. Le Guin, *Always Coming Home*

1987: Iain M. Banks, *Consider Phlebas* (Scotland)

1988: Iain M. Banks, *The Player of Games*

1988: Sheri S. Tepper, *The Gate to Women's Country* (America)

1990: Iain M. Banks, *Use of Weapons*

1990: Kim Stanley Robinson, *Pacific Edge* (America)

1991: Iain M. Banks, *The State of the Art*

1992: Francis Fukuyama *The End of History and the Last Man* (America)
—   Argued that liberal capitalism represents the culmination of sociocultural development, a viewpoint Marxist philosopher Slavoj Žižek sees as emblematic of consensus liberal ideology during the 90s. History is dead...

1992: Kim Stanley Robinson, *Red Mars*

1993: Kim Stanley Robinson, *Green Mars*

1993: Starhawk, *The Fifth Sacred* (America)

1996: Iain M. Banks, *Excession*

1996: Kim Stanley Robinson, *Blue Mars*

1997: Arthur C Clarke, *3001: The Final Odyssey*

1998: Iain M. Banks, *Inversions*

1999: Brian Aldiss and Roger Penrose, *White Mars: A 21st Century Utopia* (England)

2000: Iain M. Banks, *Look to Windward*

September 11 attacks (2001)

2001–8: Kozue Amano, *Aria* (Japan)

2003: Marshall Brain, *Manna* (America)

Financial crisis of 2007–8

Long live History! (& maybe utopia too?) With the financial collapse and liberal centrism finding itself increasingly contested, both from the right and the left, there is once again the potential for utopian literature to flourish and experience a fresh revival.

2008: Iain M. Banks, *Matter*

2010: Iain M. Banks, *Surface Detail*

2010: Alan Jaccobs, Eutopia: *The Gnostic Land of Prester John* (England)
— The title of this book is a clear allusion to Thomas More's *Utopia*.

2012: Iain M. Banks, *The Hydrogen Sonata*

2013: Lauren Groff, *Arcadia* (England)

2013: Robert Llewellyn, *News From Gardenia* (England)

2013: Robert Llewellyn, *News from the Squares*

2015: Robert Llewellyn, *News from the Clouds*
— The titles in this series are a clear allusion to William Morris's *News from Nowhere*

2016: Ada Palmer, *Too Like the Lightning* (America)

2016: Kim Stanley Robinson, 'Mutt and Jeff Push the Button' (short story)

2016: Nisi Shawl, *Everfair* (America)
— The greatest of the contemporary utopias, and the only 'historical what-if' (or counterfactual) utopia I have encountered. This book reimagines the Belgium Congo as a free utopia, with extensive references made to The Fabian Society.

2016: Neal Shusterman, *Scythe* (America)

2017: Cory Doctorow, *Walkaway* (England)

2017: Phil Kelly, *Farsight: Crisis of Faith* (England)
— Set in the highly dystopic mythos of the miniature war game, Warhammer 40,000, this novel depicts one of the few utopian factions, the Tau, whose social organisation contains utopian and dystopian elements and is semi-modelled on Plato's Republic. Even in popular culture, utopias continue to exercise a power over the imagination.

2018: Lizette Agenbach, *Utopia* (South Africa)
— The title of this book is a clear allusion to Thomas More's *Utopia*.

2018: Liza Daly, *Harmonia* (interactive story) (America)
— Can be played online

2018 Neal Shusterman, *Thunderhead* (America)

2019: Erik Hinton *Your World Is Going to Shatter*

Recommended Reading

Utopias

Early

Thomas More, *Utopia* (Verso, 2016 edition with essays by Ursula K. Le Guin and China Miéville)

Johannes Valentinus Andreae, *Christianopolis* (Cosimo Classics, 2007 edition translated and introduced by Felix Emil Held)

Gregory Claeys (ed.) (anthology), *Utopias of the British Enlightenment*

Modern

Edward Bellamy, *Looking Backward: 2000-1887*

William Morris, *News from Nowhere*

Edward Carpenter (poetry), 'Towards Democracy'

H. G. Wells, *A Modern Utopia*

Charlotte Perkins Gilman, *Herland*

Contemporary

Ursula K. Le Guin, *The Dispossessed*

Marge Piercy, *Woman on the Edge of Time*

Iain M. Banks, *Consider Phlebas*

Kim Stanley Robinson, *Mars Trilogy*

Nisi Shawl, *Everfair*

Nonfiction

Literary Theory

Michael Robertson, *The Last Utopians*

Gregory Claeys (ed), *The Cambridge Companion to Utopian Literature*

Krishan Kumar, *Utopianism*

Radical Utopianism

A.L. Morton, The English Utopia (available free at *marxist.org*)

McKenzie Wark, *Molecular Red*

Peter Hudis, *Marx's Concept of the Alternative to Capitalism*

Notes

1   Lyman Tower Sargent, *Utopianism: A Very Short Introduction* (Oxford: OUP, 2010), Ebook.
2   Karl Marx & Friedrich Engels, *The German Ideology* (New York: Prometheus Books, 1998), p.57.
3   Thomas More, *Utopia* (London: Folio Society, 2011).
4   Fátima Vieira, 'The concept of utopia' in Gregory Claeys (ed), *The Cambridge Companion to Utopian Literature* (New York: CUP, 2010), p.3.
5   Anis S. Bawarshi and Mary Jo Reiff, *Genre* (West Lafayette: Parlor Press, 2010), pp.212, 4.
6   Margaret Atwood, *In Other Worlds* (London: Virago, 2011) Ebook, p.7.
7   Roland Barthes, *Image Music Text* (London: Fontana Press, 1997), p.160.
8   Michel Foucault, *The Archaeology of Knowledge* (Oxford: Routledge, 2002), p.211.
9   Nicole Pohl, 'Utopianism after More' in Gregory Claeys (ed), *The Cambridge Companion to Utopian Literature* (New York: CUP, 2010), p.56.
10   Susan Bruce (ed), *Three Early Modern Utopias* (Oxford: OUP, 2010), p.xiii.
11   Vieira, p.7.
12   Krishan Kumar, *Utopianism* (Bristol: Open University Press, 1991), p.29.
13   Karl Mannheim, quoted in Paul Ricœur, *Lectures on Ideology and Utopia* (New York: Columbia University Press, 1986), p.173.
14   Kumar, pp.17, 27.
15   Atwood, *Worlds*, p.59.
16   Kumar, p.35.
17   Tao Yuanming, Gladys Yang (Trans.), *Selected Poems* (Beijing: Panda Books, 1993), p.91.
18   Plato, *Republic*, in Cooper, John M., *Complete Works* (Indianapolis: Hackett Publishing, 1997).

19   Tacitus 'Germanica' in John Carey, *The Faber Book of Utopias* (London: Faber & Faber, 1999).

20   John Carey, *The Faber Book of Utopias* (London: Faber & Faber, 1999) p.v.

21   Augustine, Saint of Hippo, *City of God* (London: Folio, 2012).

22   Thomas Aquinas, *Commentary on Aristotle's Politics* (Indianapolis: Hackett Publishing, 2007).

23   Sargent, Utopianism, Ebook.

24   Quentin Skinner 'Sir Thomas More's Utopia' in Anthony Pagden (ed), *The Languages of Political Theory in Early-Modern* Europe (Cambridge: CUP, 1987), p.125.

25   Peter Berglar, *Thomas More: A Lonely Voice Against the Power of the State*, (Cologne, Scepter, 2010), Ebook.

26   Kumar, p.39.

27   Iain M. Banks, *Consider Phlebas* (London: Hachette Digital, 2008) Ebook, p.498.

28   Haywire Mac, *The Big Rock Candy Mountains* in Ross Bradshaw (ed), *Utopia* (Nottingham: Five Leaves, 2012), p.197.

29   Samuel R. Delany, *Triton* (London: Gollancz, 2013) Ebook.

30   Michael Piller, 'Ensign Ro' (*Star Trek: The Next Generation*) (1991, http://www.chakoteya.net/nextgen/203.htm [22/11/15]).

31   Anonymous, *Bestiary* (London: Folio Society, 1992); Robert Lewis Stevenson, *Strange Case of Dr. Jekyll and Mr. Hyde* in John Wain (ed), *The Oxford Library of Short Novels* (London: Guild Publishing, 1990); Mary Shelley, *Frankenstein* (London: Folio Society, 2004).

32   William Gibson, Neuromancer (London: Voyager, 2010) Ebook, p.193.

33   Darko Suvin, 'Cognition and Estrangement' in Suman Gupta and David Johnson, *A Twentieth-century Literature Reader* (Abingdon-on-Thames: Routledge, 2005), p.188.

34   Bertolt Brecht, *Brecht on Theatre* (London: Methuen, 1964), p.143.

35   Theodore Sturgeon, *More Than Human* (Guernsey: Gollancz, 2000).

36   Slavoj Žižek, *Living in the End Times* (London: Verso, 2011), p.376.

37   Jacqueline Dutton, '"Non-western" utopian traditions' in Gregory Claeys (ed), *The Cambridge Companion to Utopian Literature* (New York: CUP, 2010), p.223.

38   E. M. Forster, *The Eternal Moment and Other Short Stories* (New York: Harvest Book, 1970).

39   John Wyndham, *The Chrysalids* (London: Folio Society, 2010).

40   Walter M. Miller, Jr., *A Canticle for Leibowitz* (London: Orbit, 1993).

41   Russell Hoban, *Riddley Walker* (London: Bloomsbury, 2002).

42   Margaret Atwood, *Oryx and Crake* (London: Bloomsbury, 2003), *The Year of the Flood*, (London: Bloomsbury, 2009), *MaddAddam* (London: Virago, 2014).

43   Dmitry Glukhovsky, *Metro 2033* (London: Orion, 2009).

44   Sheri S. Tepper, *The Gate to Women's Country* (London: Gollancz, 2011) Ebook.

45   Mary Shelley, *The Last Man* (London: Folio Society, 2012).

46   Friedrich Engels, *Socialism, Utopian and Scientific (Classic Reprint)* (London: Forgotten Books, 2012).

47   Thomas Hobbes, *Leviathan* (Cambridge: CUP, 2006).

48   Gerrard Winstanley, *'The True Levellers' Standard Advanced', 'The Law of Freedom' and Other Writings* (Luxemburg: CreateSpace, 2014).

49   John Locke, *Two Treatises of Government and A Letter Concerning Toleration* (Luxemburg: CreateSpace, 2011).

50   James Harrington, *The Commonwealth of Oceana* (2013, http://www.gutenberg.org/files/2801/2801-h/2801-h.htm [25/11/14]).

51   Edmund Burke, *Reflections on the Revolution in France (Oxford World's Classics)* (Oxford: OUP, 2009).

52   Jean-Jacques Rousseau, *The Social Contract* (London: Penguin, 1971).

53   William Godwin, *Enquiry Concerning Political Justice* (Oxford: OUP, 2013).

54   Thomas Malthus, *An Essay on the Principle of Population (Oxford World's Classics)* (New York: OUP, 1993).

55   Charlotte Perkins Gilman, 'Moving the Mountain' in *The Herland Trilogy* (New York: Start Publishing, 2012) Ebook.

56   Paul Ricœur, *Lectures on Ideology and Utopia* (New York: Columbia University Press, 1986), p.6.

57   J. B. S. Haldane, *Daedalus; or, Science and the Future* (1993, http://vserver1.cscs.lsa.umich.edu/~crshalizi/ Daedalus.html [27/11/14]).

58   Walter Houghton, *The Victorian Frame of Mind, 1830-1870* (London: Yale University Press, 1985), p.27.

59   Étienne Cabet, *Voyage to Icaria* (New York: Syracuse University Press, 2003).

60   Edward Bellamy, *Looking Backward: 2000-1887* (New York: Penguin, 2002) Ebook.

61   Marge Piercy, *Woman on the Edge of Time* (London: The Woman's Press, 1979).

62   Deirdre O'Byrne 'Woman on the Edge of Time' in Bradshaw, p.78.

63   D. B. Fenlon, 'England and Europe: *Utopia* and its aftermath' in 'Transactions of the Royal Historical Society, 25' (1975, http://journals.cambridge.org/action/ displayAbstract?fromPage=online&aid=3465840&fulltextT ype=RA&fileId=S0080440100018065, [19/5/15]), p.122.

64   Nathaniel Hawthorne, *The Blithedale Romance* (New York: OUP, 2009), p.16.

65   Kumar, p.2.

66   Noam Chomsky, *Occupy* (London: Penguin, 2012), Ebook.

67   'Awra Amba: an Ethiopian utopia? – video' (http:// www.theguardian.com/global-development/video/2014/ apr/15/awra-amba-ethiopian-utopia-video?CMP=fb_gu, [25/3/15]).

68   Dan Hancox, *The Village Against the World* (London: Verso, 2013), p.13.

69   David Cameron has been linked to philosopher Philip Blond Red Toryism and Catholic Radical Orthodoxy. G.K. Chesterton and Hilaire Belloc shaped Blond's neo-Distributism; in the term of an unsympathetic commentary from the Marxist Richard Seymour, for 'an artisanal Arcadia'. This ideology is revolutionary and, 'explicitly

utopian in its foundation.' Richard Seymour, *The Meaning of David Cameron* (Winchester: O-Books, 2010), p.77.

70   David Pearce, 'The Hedonistic Imperative' (http://www.hedweb.com, [25/3/15]).

71   Peter Hudis, *Marx's Concept of the Alternative to Capitalism* (Chicago: Haymarket Books, 2013), p. 157

72   Peter Hudis, pp. 176, 123, 182.

73   Ursula K. Le Guin, *The Dispossessed* (London: Orion, 2002), p.7.

74   Philip K. Dick, *The Man in the High Castle* (London: Folio Society, 2015), p.39.

75   David Hume 'Idea of a Perfect Commonwealth' in Gregory Claeys (ed), *Utopias of the British Enlightenment* (New York: CUP, 1994), p.58.

76   William Morris, *News from Nowhere and Other Writings* (London: Penguin 1993) Ebook.

77   Bawarshi and Reiff, p.20.

78   Aldous Huxley, *Island* (London: Flamingo, 1994), pp.80, 67, 42, 97, 213, 218.

79   Skinner, pp.123, 124.

80   Peter Ackroyd in Thomas More, *Utopia* (London: Folio Society, 2011), p.xiii-xiv.

81   Clive Wilmer in William Morris, *News from Nowhere and Other Writings* (London: Penguin 1993) Ebook.

82   D. B. Fenlon, 'England and Europe: *Utopia* and its aftermath' in 'Transactions of the Royal Historical Society, 25' (1975, http://journals.cambridge.org/action/displayAbstract?fromPage=online&aid=3465840&fulltextType=RA&fileId=S0080440100018065, [19/5/15]), pp.124, 126.

83   Adam Roberts, *Fredric Jameson (Routledge Critical Thinkers)* (London: Routledge, 2001) Ebook.

84   Fredric Jameson, *Archaeologies of the Future* (London: Verso, 2007), p.50.

85   Kumar, p.45.

86   Tommaso Campanella 'The City of the Sun' in *Famous Utopias* (New York: Hendricks House, 1955).

87   Robert Burton, *The Anatomy of Melancholy* (Oxford: Benediction Classics, 2016)

88   Kumar quoting J. Max Patrick's view on Robert Burton
      and Kumar's own summary, p.46.
89   Samuel Butler, *Erewhon* (London: Penguin, 1985).
90   H. G. Wells, A Modern Utopia (London: Penguin, 2005).
91   Eric Hobsbawm, *How to Change the World: Tales of Marx
      and Marxism* (London: Little, Brown Book Group, 2011)
      Ebook, p.17.
92   Lymon Tower Sargent 'Colonial and postcolonial utopias'
      in Gregory Claeys (ed), *The Cambridge Companion to
      Utopian Literature* (New York: CUP, 2010), p.205.
93   Pohl, p.58.
94   Johannes Valentinus Andreae, *Christianopolis* (New York:
      Cosimo, 2007).
95   Giovanni Botero, *The Reason of State* (New Haven: Yale
      University Press, 1956).
96   Mark Goldie, 'The civil religion of James Harrington' in
      Anthony Pagden (ed), *The Languages of Political Theory in
      Early-Modern Europe* (Cambridge: CUP, 1987), p.206.
97   François Rabelais 'Gargantua and Pantagruel' in François
      Rabelais, *The Collected Works of François Rabelais* (London:
      University of California Press, 1999), p.126.
98   Margaret Cavendish, *The Blazing World and Other Writings*
      (London: Penguin, 1994) Ebook.
99   Pohl, p.62.
100   Pohl, p.55.
101   Francis Bacon 'New Atlantis' in Susan Bruce (ed), *Three
      Early Modern Utopias* (Oxford: OUP, 2010), p.177.
102   Daniel Defoe, *Robinson Crusoe* (London: Folio Society,
      1972).
103   Sargent, Utopianism, Ebook.
104   Anonymous, 'The Island of Content: or, A New Paradise
      Discovered' in Claeys, *Utopias.*
105   Anonymous, 'A Description of New Athens in Terra
      Australis Incognita' in Claeys, *Utopias.*
106   Robert Paltock, 'The Life and Adventures of Peter Wilkins'
      in John Carey, *The Faber Book of Utopias* (London: Faber &
      Faber, 1999).
107   Samuel Johnson, 'Rasselas' in John Carey, *The Faber Book of
      Utopias* (London: Faber & Faber, 1999).

108 Vieira, p.10.

109 H. J. Anderson, *Mundus Alter et Idem* (London: George Bell & Sons, 1908)

110 Pohl, pp.62-3.

111 Kenneth M. Roemer, 'Paradise transformed' in Gregory Claeys (ed), *The Cambridge Companion to Utopian Literature* (New York: CUP, 2010), p.80.

112 Mikhail Bakhtin, *The Dialogic Imagination: Four Essays (University of Texas Press Slavic Series)* (Austin: University of Texas Press, 1981) Ebook.

113 Voltaire, *Candide and Other Stories*, (Oxford: OUP, 2006) Ebook.

114 Sargent, Utopianism, Ebook.

115 Jonathan Swift, *Gulliver's Travels* (Berwick-upon-Tweed: Folio Society, 2011).

116 George Orwell, *Animal Farm*, (London: Folio Society, 1984).

117 Sargent, Utopianism, Ebook.

118 Pohl, p.63.

119 Henry Neville 'The Isle of the Pines' in Susan Bruce (ed), *Three Early Modern Utopias* (Oxford: OUP, 2010), p.198.

120 David Hume 'Idea of a Perfect Commonwealth' in Claeys, *Utopias*, p.58.

121 Kumar, pp.68-9.

122 Anonymous, 'Bruce's Voyage to Naples' in Claeys, *Utopias*.

123 Edward Bulwer-Lytton 'The Coming Race' in John Carey, *The Faber Book of Utopias* (London: Faber & Faber, 1999).

124 Marquis de Sade, *Justine, Philosophy in the Bedroom, & Other Writings* (New York: Grove Press, 1990).

125 Pierre Klossowski, *Sade my Neighbour* (Evanston, Northwestern University Press, 1991), p.52.

126 Atwood, *Worlds*, p.66.

127 Thomas Northmore 'Memoirs of Planetes, or a Sketch of the Laws and Manners of Makar' in Claeys, *Utopias*, pp.137, 139.

128 Atwood, *Worlds*, p.81.

129 W. H. Hudson, *A Crystal Age* (Whitefish: Kessinger, 2011).

130 Ignatius Donnelly, *Cæsar's Column: a Story of the Twentieth-century* (Lenox: HardPress, 2014) Ebook.

131 William Dean Howells, *A Traveller from Altruria* (Whitefish: Kessinger, 2010).

132 Edward Bellamy, *Equality: The Stunning Sequel to Looking Backward* (Rockville: Wildside Press, 2010).

133 Edward Bellamy, *Looking Backward: 2000–1887* (New York: Penguin, 2002) Ebook, p.24.

134 William Morris, *News from Nowhere and Other Writings* (London: Penguin 1993) Ebook, p.357.

135 Bellamy, *Backwards*, p.59

136 Morris, *News*, p.324, p.356

137 Bellamy, *Backwards*, p.100, p.81, p.123, p.31, p.109, p.30, p.48, p.39, p.51

138 Morris, *News*, p.295, p.296, p.123, p.183

139 Gregory Claeys, 'The origins of dystopia' in Gregory Claeys (ed), *The Cambridge Companion to Utopian Literature* (New York: CUP, 2010), p.108.

140 W.H. Auden, 'Vespers' in Encounter (1955, http://www.unz.org/Pub/Encounter-1955feb-00010 [19/5/15].

141 Claeys, p.109.

142 Yevgeny Zamyatin, *We* (New York: Penguin, 1993).

143 Jack London: *The Iron Heel* (New York: Penguin, 2006).

144 Aristophanes, *The Birds and Other Plays* (London: Penguin, 1978).

145 Aristophanes, *Lysistrata and Other Plays* (London: Penguin, 1973).

146 H. G. Wells, *A Modern Utopia* (London: Penguin, 2005), pp. 12, 64.

147 Gabriel Tarde, 'Underground Man' in John Carey, *The Faber Book of Utopias* (London: Faber & Faber, 1999).

148 Charlotte Perkins Gilman, *The Yellow Wall-Paper, Herland, and Selected Writings* (London Penguin, 1999).

149 Charlotte Perkins Gilman, 'Moving the Mountain' in *The Herland Trilogy* (New York: Start Publishing, 2012) Ebook.

150 Austin Tappan Wright, *Islandia* (New York: Overlook Press, 2007).

151 Kumar, p.40.

152 B. F. Skinner, *Walden Two* (Indianapolis: Hackett, 2005) Ebook, p.9

153 H. P. Lovecraft, 'At the Mountains of Madness' in H. P. Lovecraft, *Necronomicon*, (London: Gollancz, 2008), p.471.

154 Vieira, pp.17-8.

155 Sargent, *Cambridge Companion to Utopian Literature:* p.209.

156 Peter Fitting, 'Utopia, dystopia and science fiction' in Gregory Claeys (ed), *The Cambridge Companion to Utopian Literature* (New York: CUP, 2010), p.150.

157 Sarah Scott, *Millennium Hall* (Toronto: Broadview Press, 2001).

158 Alessa Johns, 'Feminism and utopianism' in Gregory Claeys (ed), *The Cambridge Companion to Utopian Literature* (New York: CUP, 2010), pp.174, 178.

159 Elizabeth Burgoyne Corbett, *New Amazonia: A Foretaste of the Future* (Seattle: Aqueduct Press, 2014) Ebook.

160 Mary Bradley Lane, *Mizora* (Lincoln: University of Nebraska Press, 1999).

161 Joanna Russ, *The Female Man* (London: Gollancz, 2010) Ebook.

162 John Wyndham, *Consider Her Ways and Others* (London: Penguin, 1983).

163 Charlotte Perkins Gilman, *The Yellow Wall-Paper, Herland, and Selected Writings* (London: Penguin, 1999), p.271.

164 Rokeya Sakhawat Hussain, *Sultana's Dream and Padramarag* (London: Penguin, 2005).

165 Ursula K. Le Guin, *Worlds of Exile and Illusion*, (New York: St Martin's Press, 2007).

166 Ursula K. Le Guin, *The Left Hand of Darkness* (London: Hachette Digital, 2012) Ebook.

167 Ursula K. Le Guin, *The Dispossessed* (London: Orion, 2002), p.139.

168 Fitting, p.145.

169 Marge Piercy, *Woman on the Edge of Time* (London: The Woman's Press, 1979), p.35.

170 Ernest Callenbach, *Ecotopia* (New York: Bantam Books, 2009) Ebook.

171 Brian Stableford, 'Ecology and dystopia' in Gregory Claeys (ed), *The Cambridge Companion to Utopian Literature* (New York: CUP, 2010), p.274.

172   Ernest Callenbach, *Ecotopia* (New York: Bantam Books, 2009) Ebook, p.164.

173   Ernest Callenbach, *Ecotopia Emerging* (Kent Town: Banyan Tree Book Distributor, 1981).

174   Kim Stanley Robinson, *Red Mars* (London: Voyager Classics, 2013); *Green Mars* (London: Voyager Classics, 2013); *Blue Mars* (London: Voyager Classics, 2013) Ebook, p.699.

175   Brian Aldiss and Roger Penrose, *White Mars: A 21st Century Utopia* (London: Sphere, 2000), p.323.

176   Ben Okri, *The Age of Magic* (London: Head of Zeus, 2014), p.29.

177   Chuck Palahniuk, *Fight Club* (London: Vintage, 2005).

178   Slavoj Žižek in Eric Dean Rasmussen, 'Liberation Hurts: An Interview with Slavoj Žižek' (2004, http://www.electronicbookreview.com/thread/endconstruction/desublimation [30/11/14]).

179   Andrey Platonov, *Soul* (London: Vintage, 2013) Ebook.

180   Mario Vargas Llosa, *The War of the End of the World* (London: Faber and Faber, 2012) Ebook.

181   Toni Morrison, *Paradise* (London: Vintage, 2010) Ebook.

182   Mario Vargas Llosa, *The War of the End of the World* (London: Faber and Faber, 2012) Ebook, p.36.

183   Llosa, *The War of the End of the World*, p.91.

184   Toni Morrison, *Paradise*, p.177.

185   Ray Bradbury, *Fahrenheit 451* (London: Folio Society, 2011).

186   William Golding, *Lord of the Flies* (London: Folio Society, 2009).

187   William F. Nolan and George Clayton Johnson, *Logan's Run* (New York: Buccaneer, 1992).

188   Philip K. Dick, *Do Androids Dream of Electric Sheep?* (London: Gollancz, 2004).

189   Anthony Burgess, *A Clockwork Orange* (London: Folio Society, 2014), Anthony Burgess, *1985*, (London: Serpent Tail, 2013) Ebook.

190   Ira Levin, *This Perfect Day* (London: Corsair, 2014) Ebook.

191   Stephen King, *The Running Man*, (London: New England Library, 2007) Ebook.

192 Margaret Atwood, *The Handmaid's Tale* (London: Folio Society, 2012).

193 P. D. James, *The Children of Men* (London: Faber and Faber, 2008) Ebook.

194 Claeys, p.114.

195 Katherine Burdekin, *Swastika Night* (New York: The Feminist Press, 1985).

196 Aldous Huxley, *Brave New World* (London: Folio Society, 2013).

197 George Orwell, *Nineteen Eighty-Four* (London: Folio Society, 2001).

198 H. G. Wells, *The Sleeper Awakes* (London: Penguin, 2005), p.102.

199 Claeys, p.118.

200 Kumar, p.90.

201 Ricœur, *Time*, vol. 3, p.258.

202 Scott Westerfeld, *Uglies Quartet: Uglies; Pretties; Specials: Extras* (London: Simon & Schuster, 2013) Ebook.

203 Suzanne Collins, *The Hunger Games Complete Trilogy (Hunger Games Trilogy)* (London: Scholastic Books, 2013) Ebook.

204 James Dashner, *The Maze Runner Complete Collection* (Frome: Chicken House, 2013) Ebook.

205 Veronica Roth, *Divergent Trilogy (books 1-3)* (London: HarperCollins, 2013) Ebook.

206 Scott Westerfeld, *Uglies Quartet: Uglies; Pretties; Specials: Extras* (London: Simon & Schuster, 2013) Ebook.

207 Brigid Rose, *The City of Lists* (London: Crocus, 2009).

208 Kazuo Ishiguro, *Never Let Me Go* (London: Folio Society, 2012).

209 Haruki Murakami, *1Q84* (London: Harvil Seeker, 2011).

210 Howard Jacobson, *J: A Novel* (London: Jonathan Cape, 2014) Ebook.

211 Jasper Fforde, *Shades of Grey: The Road to High Saffron* (London: Hodder & Stoughton, 2010) Ebook.

212 David Mitchell, *Cloud Atlas* (St Ives: Sceptre, 2004).

213 Doris Lessing, *Shikasta* (London: Fourth Estate, 2012); *The Marriages Between Zones 3, 4 and 5,* (London: Fourth

Estate, 2012); *The Sirian Experiments* (London: Fourth
Estate, 2012); *The Making of the Representative for Planet 8*
(London: Fourth Estate, 2012); *The Sentimental Agents in
the Volyen* (London: Fourth Estate, 2012).

214   Suzy McKee Charnas, *Walk to the End of the World and
Motherlines* (London: The Women's Press, 1989).

215   *Brazil*, dir. by Terry Gilliam (Universal Studies, 1985)
[DVD].

216   *Bioshock*, dir. by Ken Levine (2K Games, 2007) [PC
Game].

217   Alan Moore, *V for Vendetta* (New York: DC Comics, 2008).

218   *Utopia*, dir. by Dennis Kelly (Kudos Film and Television,
2013) [DVD].

219   Richard Rorty, *Contingency, Irony, and Solidarity* (New
York: CUP, 1995), p.61.

220   Alasdair MacIntyre, *After Virtue* (Notre Dame: University
of Notre Dame Press, 2007), p.263.

221   Raymond Tallis, *The Raymond Tallis Reader* (Basingstoke:
Palgrave, 2000), p.188.